SWU-800- 010

UNIFORMS OF RUSSIAN ARMY DURING THE YEARS 1825-1855 VOL. 10

UNDER THE REIGN OF NICHOLAS I
EMPEROR OF RUSSIA BETWEEN 1825 TO 1855
GENERAL MAJOR STAFF, AIDE DE CAMPS & OTHERS

From the Viskovatov's greatest work:
"Historical description of the clothing and
arms of the Russian Army"

English translation by Mark Conrad

SOLDIERSHOP PUBLISHING

AUTHOR

Aleksandr Vasilevich Viskovatov born 22 April (4 May New Style) 1804, died 27 February (11 March) 1858 in St. Petersburg, Russian military historian. He graduated from the 1st Cadet Corps and served in the artillery, the hydrographic depot of the Naval Ministry, and then in the Department of Military Educational Institutions. He mainly studied historical artifacts and the histories of military units. Viskovatov's greatest work was the Historical Description of the Clothing and Arms of the Russian Army.

PUBLISHING'S NOTE

NOTE ABOUT BOOK PRINTING BEFORE 1925

LICENSES COMMONS

ACKNOWLEDGEMENTS

A Special Thanks to NYPL and other institutions for their kindly permission to use some images of his archives, collections or books used in our book.

Title: **UNIFORMS OF RUSSIAN ARMY DURING THE YEARS 1825-1855. VOL. 10**
Under the reign of Nicholas I emperor of Russia between 1825-1855
By A.V.Viskovatov. Serie edit by Luca S. Cristini. First edition by Soldiershop. May 2019
Cover & Art Design: Luca S. Cristini. Plates re-colorations by Anna Cristini. ISBN code: 978-88-93274272
Published by Luca Cristini Editore, via Orio 35/4- 24050 Zanica (BG) ITALY. www.soldiershop.com

UNIFORMS OF THE RUSSIAN ARMY DURING THE YEARS 1825-1855 VOL. 10

UNDER THE REIGN OF NICHOLAS I EMPEROUR OF RUSSIA BETWEEN 1825 AND 1855

*

GENERAL MAJOR STAFF, AIDE DE CAMPS & OTHERS

V.Adam

Aide de camp of the Emperor Nicholas I 1848 by V.Adam

HISTORICAL DESCRIPTION OF THE CLOTHING AND ARMS
OF THE RUSSIAN ARMY - A.V. VISKOVATOV
(First English translation by Mark Conrad)

Soldiershop is glad to presents the complete collection of the great job made by A.V. Viskovatov dedicated to the uniforms and weapons belonging from the first Zar and Russian emperors to the Russian army during the Napoleonic period, until 1860 about. The time we considered in this volume corresponds to the reigns of Nicholas I that was the Emperor of Russia from 1825 until 1855. He was also the King of Poland and Grand Duke of Finland. He is best known as a political conservative whose reign was marked by geographical expansion, repression of dissent, economic stagnation, poor administrative policies, a corrupt bureaucracy, and frequent wars that culminated in Russia's defeat in the Crimean War of 1853–56.

Our reprint in based on the original 19th century volumes. This part is distributed at now on six volumes.

Our new edition, the first ever published in English, both on paper and digital format, boasts a large number of color plates, many of them unpublished and re-coloured by our team of expert artists and scholars of uniformology. Each volume is based on 100 color plates or more, always accompanied by the original translated text which describes the subjets of the plates.

A unique work in its genre, a must have in any respecting collection!

Aleksandr Vasilevich Viskovatov born 22 April (4 May New Style) 1804, died 27 February (11 March) 1858 in St. Petersburg, Russian military historian. He graduated from the 1st Cadet Corps and served in the artillery, the hydrographic depot of the Naval Ministry, and then in the Department of Military Educational Institutions.

He mainly studied historical artifacts and the histories of military units. Viskovatov's greatest work was the Historical Description of the Clothing and Arms of the Russian Army (Vols. 1-30, St. Petersburg, 1841-62; 2nd ed. Vols. 1-34, St. Petersburg - Novosibirsk - Leningrad, 1899-1948). This work is based on a great quantity of archival documents and contains four thousand colored illustrations.

Viskovatov was the author of Chronicles of the Russian Army (Books 1-20, St. Petersburg, 1834-42) and Chronicles of the Russian Imperial Army (Parts 1-7, St. Petersburg, 1852). He collected valuable material on the history of the Russian navy which went into A Short Overview of Russian Naval Campaigns and General Voyages to the End of the XVII Century (St. Petersburg, 1864; 2nd edition Moscow, 1946). Together with A.I. Mikhailovskii-Danilevskii he helped prepare and create the Military Gallery in the Winter Palace.

He wrote the historical military inscriptions for the walls of the Hall of St. George in the Great Palace of the Kremlin. (From the article in the Soviet Military Encyclopedia.)

CONTENTS

*

Preface pag. 5

53 - Military Educational Institutions. Pag. 7

54 - General Officers. Pag. 16

55 - General-Adjutants & Aide de camp. Pag. 18

56 - General of Imperial Maiesty's suite. Pag. 20

*

Notes pag. 22

PLATES pag. 27

HISTORICAL DESCRIPTION OF THE CLOTHING AND ARMS OF THE RUSSIAN ARMY

General Officers, General-Adjutants and Aides-de-Camp 1825-1855

CHANGES IN THE UNIFORMS AND EQUIPMENT OF TEMPORARY FORCES FROM 1801 TO 1825.

LIII. MILITARY EDUCATIONAL INSTITUTIONS. [*Voenno-Uchebnyya zavedeniya.*]

A.) Cadet Corps and Nobiliary Regiment.

11 February 1826 – In place of the double-breasted dress coat [*mundir*], officers, pupils, and cadre lower ranks of the several cadet corps (except for the Finland Cadet Corps which kept its previous uniform), the Imperial Military Orphans' Home [*IMPERATORSKII Voenno-Sirotskii Dom*], and the Nobiliary Regiment [*Dvoryanskii polk*] were given **single-breasted coats** with red piping down the front and along the bottom to the turnbacks. Also established were long dark-green pants with red piping on the side seams, along with black cloth half-gaiters [*polushtiblety*]. All this was as introduced at this same time for all Army infantry. Generals, field-grade officers, and adjutants (for whom half-gaiters were not prescribed) were to wear boots with the spurs driven in (Illus. 893, 894, 895, and 896) (1).

11 April 1826 - The cloth base of officers' **epaulettes** and small cross-straps are to correspond to the colors of the cadets' shoulder straps: for the 1st Cadet Corps—red, the second—white, and the Nobiliary Regiment—yellow (Illus. 896) (2).

10 May 1826 - In summertime and when they must be mounted in formation, general, field-grade officers, and adjutants are to wear white linen **pants** without integral spats [*kozyrki*], just as prescribed for these ranks in all arms (Illus. 897) (3).

1 January 1827 - In order to distinguish **ranks**, officers' epaulettes are to have small forged or stamped silver stars in the same scheme as established at this time for the officers' epaulettes ina all branches and described for Grenadier regiments. Starting in this same year, pupils of the varioius Cadet corps and the Nobiliary Regiment are issued dark-green cloth jackets [*kurtki*] for everyday wear. These are patterned on the dress coat [*mundir*] but without skirts or lace, and have dark-green cuffs. Also introduced at this time are grey trousers: in winter—of cloth, in summer—of calamanco or dyed linen (Illus. 898) (4).

8 March 1828 - The **Moscow Cadet Corps** (consisting of one Grenadier company, three Musketeer companies, and a juvenile section) is prescribed for uniform clothing the same as for the 1st and 2nd Cadet Corps but with light-blue shoulder straps and base for officers' epaulettes, and without gold lace on officers' coats (Illus. 899) (5).

24 April 1828 – Officers, pupils, and all combatant lower ranks in the various cadet corps, the Imperial Military Orphans' Home, and the Nobiliary Regiment are given a new style of **shako** based on those prescribed at this time for all infantry troops. The plates for these shakos are to be higher than before and not semicircular, but instead are vertically elongated (Illus. 899) (6).

22 February 1829 – With the renaming of the Imperial Military Orphans' Home to the **Paul Cadet Corps** [*Pavlovskii Kadetskii korpus*], officers, pupils, and combatant lower ranks are to have uniforms like those of the 1st and 2nd Cadet Corps but with light-blue for shoulder straps and the base of officers' epaulettes (Illus. 900), as had been for the Moscow Cadet Corps. This last corps, though, is to have shoulder straps and the base of epaulettes in dark green, with the shoulder straps piped red (7).

16 December 1829 - In the various cadet corps and the Nobiliary Regiment the cuffs of officers' **frock coats** [*syurtuki*], instead of being red, are to be dark green with red piping (Illus. 901) (8).

26 December 1829 - Officers, pupils, and combatant lower ranks of all institutions are to have uniform **buttons** with the same design as prescribed at this time for Guards infantry and cavalry, i.e. depicting a two-headed eagle (9).

29 July 1830 - The **Finland Cadet Corps** is prescribed uniforms and arms like those of the various cadet corps in the capitals, but with the addition of light-blue plastrons. Collars, shoulder straps, cuffs, cuff flaps, turnback lining, and piping are also light blue. The eagle's shield on the shako plate and buttons is to have the coat-of-arms of the Grand Duchy of Finland (Illus. 962) (10).

20 August 1830 - Officers rapier swords [*shpagi*] are replaced with **half-sabers** [*polusabli*] with black scabbards and gilded brass mountings, as directed at this same time for Army infantry troops (Illus. 902) (11).

26 November 1831 - Generals and field and company-grade officers of the Moscow Cadet Corps are to wear **coats** as prescribed for the 1st, 2nd, and Paul Cadet Corps, i.e. with gold ring-shaped lace (12).

16 December 1831 - In order to differentiate pupils in all the cadet corps and the Nobiliary Regiment, it is ordered that the **shoulder straps** of coats and jackets have narrow gold lace: for sergeants [*fel'dfebeli*]—sewn on around the edges and down the center (Illus. 903 and 904a); for senior non-commissioned officers [*starshie unter-ofitsery*]—around the edges (Illus. 904b); for junior non-commissioned officers [*mladshie unter-ofitsery*]—down the center (Illus. 904c); and for lance-corporals [*yefreitory*]—across, near the lower edge (Illus. 904d). Additionally, sergeants are directed to have silver swordknots (13).

8 June 1832 - Generals and field and company-grade officers of the various cadet corps and Nobiliary Regiment are permitted to wear **moustaches** (14).

16 November 1832 - The table of uniforms and accouterments for the **Alexander Boys' Cadet Corps** [*Aleksandrovskii Maloletnyi Kadetskii korpus*] is confirmed, according to which the cadets are prescribed the following clothing: jacket [*kurtka*] of dark-green cloth, without a collar, piped red, with the same buttons as for the various combatant corps; winter trousers of grey cloth with a bib [*nagrudnik*] of the same material, with red piping on the side seams; summer trousers of white Flemish linen (white demicotton for holidays) with a similar bib; greatcoat of grey cloth, with red cloth collar and cuffs, and the same buttons as on the jacket; polished half-boots. When wearing the jacket, as well as when wearing the great coat, the reinforced linen collar of the shirt is to be let out, showing the lace edges. For all cadets the forage cap is directed to be dark green in color with a black lacquered leather visor and the cut-out letters A. K. backed with yellow on the cap band. For the first three companies, as prescribed for army cadet corps, the cap band and piping around the top of the crown are red, while in the fourth company, designated for the Naval Cadet Corps, the cap band is dark green with two white lines of piping and another line around the top of the crown (Illus. 905) (15).

22 November 1832 - For the cadets of the **Paul Cadet Corps**, the **shako pompons** and **swordknots** are to be as for the third battalions of infantry (16).

24 November 1832 - Officers, cadets, and combatant lower ranks of the various **provincial cadet corps** are to have uniforms like those of the Nobiliary Regiment but with dark-green cuff flaps with red piping, instead of red cuff flaps (17).

22 December 1832 - **Shoulder straps** for the provincial cadet corps are to be as follows: Novgorod—red; Tambov—green; Polotsk—white; and Tula—light blue (18).

3 January 1833 – Cloth **half-gaiters** were abolished for officers, pupils, and combatant lower ranks of the several cadet corps and the Nobiliary Regiment. For non-commissioned officers, lance-corporals, cadet privates, and lower ranks, **sword knots** are abolished (Illus. 906) (19).

20 February 1833 - In the various cadet corps and the Nobiliary Regiment the **summer pants** with buttons and integral spats are replaced with trousers without buttons or spats (Illus. 907) (20).

25 February 1833 - The **jackets** for classroom and everyday wear by cadets in the provincial cadet corps are to be like the jackets of the corps in the capitals, with a red cloth collar, green piping, and shoulder straps as follows: Novgorod Corps—red with green piping; Polotsk—white; Tula—light blue; and Tambov—green, these last three being with red piping (21).

16 March 1833 – The field of officers' **epaulettes** in provincial cadet corps is to be the same color as the cadets' shoulder straps (22).

5 May 1834 - Officers, cadets, and lower ranks of the **Novgorod Graf Arakcheev Cadet Corps** (renamed from the Novgorod Cadet Corps) are directed to have the Cyrillic letters G. and A. on the shoulder straps, with the first having them embroidered in silver and the rest having them cut out and backed with yellow cloth (23).

16 July 1834 - In the various cadet corps the upper and lower **pompons** are to be as for infantry regiments:

a.) In the 1st Cadet, 1st Moscow, and Novgorod Graf Arakcheev Corps—as for first battalions, namely: for Grenadier platoons—red lower pompons; Rifle platoons—yellow upper and lower pompons; Musketeer companies—white upper pompons, lower pompons white with a green center.

b.) In the 2nd Cadet, 2nd Moscow, and Polotsk Corps—as for second battalions, namely: for Grenadier platoons—lower pompons black with red below; Rifle platoons—upper and lower pompons black with yellow below; Musketeer companies—upper pompons black with white below, lower pompons white with a black center.

c.) In the Paul, Tula, and Kiev Corps—as for third battalions, namely: for Grenadier platoons—lower pompons red with light blue below; Rifle platoons—upper and lower pompons yellow with light blue below; Musketeer companies—upper pompons white with light blue below, lower pompons light blue with a white center.

d.) In the Tambov, Poltava, and Siberian Corps—as for fourth battalions, namely: for Grenadier platoons—lower pompons light blue with red below; Rifle platoons—upper and lower pompons light blue with yellow below; Musketeer companies—upper pompons light blue with white below, lower pompons white with a light blue center (24).

(Of the listed corps, the 2nd Moscow, Kiev, and Poltava were projected to be established, while the Siberian was intended to be a reorganization of the school [*uchilishche*] of the Siberian Line Cossack Host.)

26 September 1834 - When going into and breaking camp during the summer, cadets, who since 1826 have shako covers and knapsacks as the infantry, are to likewise wear the **knapsack** on two straps crossing over the chest and not on two shoulder straps and one horizontal chest-strap (Illus. 908) (25).

12 January 1835 - Pupils of the several cadet corps and the Nobiliary regiment who are designated to graduate as officers of Army Cavalry regiments or the Horse Artillery and who are detached for six months to learn service norms in the **Model Cavalry Regiment** or the **Model Horse Artillery Battery** are directed to wear: cadet shakos with cavalry cords and pompons (white for the Regiment and red for the Battery); grey cloth trousers [*reituzy*] with red piping on the side seams and leather reinforcement; and cavalry sabers with whitened cavalry sword belts worn over the coat (Illus. 909) (26). At this same time shoulder straps of coats, jackets, and greatcoats in the cadet corps as well as officers' shoulder straps are ordered to have numbers and Cyrillic letters as follows (on shoulder straps—cut out and backed with yellow cloth; on epaulettes—of embroidered silver): for the 1st Cadet Corps—1. K., 2nd Cadet—2.K., Paul—P. K., Novgorod Graf Arakcheev, as before—G. A., 1st Moscow—1. M., 2nd Moscow—2. M., Tula—T. K., Tambov—T. K., Polotsk—P. K., Kazan—K. K., Kiev—K. K., and Poltava—P. K.

21 March 1835 - Pupils from **Caucasian mountain tribes** and **Muslim** pupils, sent to the various cadet corps and the Nobiliary Regiment for education in the sciences, are prescribed the following uniform:

a.) Pupils from the mountain tribes.

1.) *Parade uniform*—Circassian caftan [*kaftan*] of light-blue cloth, with black velvet loops sewn onto the chest of the caftan near the shoulder for cartridges, called *napatroniki*, in which are placed small black cartridges with white bone caps [*nabaldashniki*] fastened to small silver plates by silver cords; *beshmet* coat of white demicotton; *sharavary* trousers of dark-green cloth; belt of red morocco leather with niello silver fittings: buckle, clasp, tip, and plate; *shapka* headdress with a white cloth crown surrounded by a black astrakhan body. Of the items listed here, the caftan, cartridge loops, *sharavary*, belt and *shapka* are trimmed with various sizes of lace. This lace is silver along the edges and gold down the center, with the silver lengths having a black silk checker pattern on the edges (Illus. 910).

2.) *Everyday uniform*—caftan and sharavary of dark-green cloth, trimmed with narrow silver lace with a black silk checker pattern along the edges. In addition, the caftan has morocco cartridge loops; *beshmet* of black demicotton with a similarly colored bast lining; black leather belt with a silvered buckle, clasp, and tip; forage cap of the usual military style, of dark-green cloth, with a red cloth band and similarly colored piping around the top (Illus. 910).

b.) Muslim pupils.

1.) *Parade uniform*—caftan of light-blue cloth, with slit sleeves; *beshmet* of yellow woolen material—both caftan and *beshmet* trimmed with the same lace as on the clothing for pupils from mountain tribes; *sharavary* trousers of dark-blue cloth; yellow silk sash; high *shapka* headdress of black astrakhan, with a pointed top of white and raspberry bands and dotted with multicolored tracery in the form of flowers (Illus. 911).

2.) *Everyday uniform*—caftan of dark-green cloth, trimmed with the same lace as on the parade uniform; *beshmet* of yellow woolen material; a silk, dark-raspberry colored bib (under the *beshmet*), trimmed around the collar with the same lace as on the caftan; *sharavary* of dark-green cloth; red leather belt with steel buckle, clasp, and tip, trimmed on the edges with narrow silver lace with black silk checks; and a dark-blue cloth forage cap with a red cloth band and red piping (Illus. 911). Black neckcloths and boots are stipulated for all four orders of dress, while for cold and inclement weather there are the normal uniform greatcoats with shoulder straps as prescribed for the particular institution (27).

20 August 1835 - Officers are to wear the **knapsack** (when in camp) in the same way as officers in all infantry units, using only two straps over the shoulders. The former horizontal strap, or chest strap, is abolished (Illus. 912) (28).

24 February 1836 - Pupils of the various cadet corps and the Nobiliary Regiment who are nominated for promotion to officers but who elect to remain at their institution are directed to have a **gold lace chevron** sewn onto the left coat sleeve (29).

21 October 1836 - Officers' saddles are to have dark-green girths with red stripes. In this same year officers' shabracks are given silver stars as in the Guards (30).

15 July 1837 - Approval is given to the new pattern of officers' **sash**, identical with that introduced at this time for all arms and described above in detail for Grenadier regiments (31).

17 December 1837 - Approval is given to a new pattern of officers' **epaulettes** with the addition of a fourth twist of thin cord (32).

15 March 1838 – The **Finland Cadet Corps** is prescribed a uniform like that of capital cadet corps, keeping only the Duchy of Finland's coat-of-arms on the shako plate and buttons. Shoulder straps and upper and lower pompons remain the same light blue as before, but with the addition of the Cyrillic letters F. K. in yellow on the straps (33).

7 June 1840 - With the ending of the practice of attaching Military Educational Institution pupils who have graduated as officers in the Horse Artillery to the **Model Horse Artillery Battery**, the uniform prescribed for those persons on 12 January 1835 is abolished (34).

2 January 1844 - Officers are to have an oval metallic **cockade** on the cap band of the forage cap, of the same colors as the cockades on officers' hats (Illus. 913) (35).

9 May 1844 - In place of shakos, officers, cadets, and combatant lower ranks of the several cadet corps and the Nobiliary Regiment are given **helmets** with the same plates as before but otherwise the same in all details as the helmets received at this time by combatant ranks in the infantry (Illus. 914 and 915) (36).

4 June 1844 - The **Orenburg-Nepluev Cadet Corps** is prescribed the following uniform in the cossack style:

a.) *Cadets*—dark-green jacket with identical dark-green edging to the red collar, dark-green cuffs piped red, scaled brass epaulettes on a light-blue base and having attached the white metal Cyrillic letters O. N., and a two-headed eagle on the buttons as for other cadet corps; dark-green *sharavary* trousers with single red stripes; light-blue girdle; *shapka* headdress with a red bag, brass cadet plate, white lower pompon, and white upper pompon (Illus. 916). With this uniform is prescribed a *shashka* sword on a red leather swordbelt and a cartridge pouch with a three-flamed grenade, on a white belt. The classroom or everyday uniform consists of: jacket without epaulettes but with light-blue shoulder straps on which are cut out the letters O. N. backed by yellow cloth; *sharavary* without stripes; and a dark-green forage cap with a red band and piping (Illus. 917). The greatcoat is grey with the same shoulder straps as on the jacket.

b.) *Officers*—dark-green *chekmen* tunic with similarly colored collar and cuffs, as for cadets, and with scaled gilt epaulettes. All else is as for cadets with the usual officers' distinctions, among them the sash and common cossack-style ammunition pouch [*patrontash*] (Illus. 917) (37).

7 December 1844 - When not on duty and when wearing the uniform coat of the institution to which are assigned, **generals** of the various cadet corps and the Nobiliary Regiment are to have white plumes on their hats instead of black (38).

4 January 1845 - Officers' helmets are to have a metal **cockade** on the right side under the chinscales, as laid down at this time for the rest of the army (39).

9 August 1845 - When in camp dress the helmets are to be worn without plumes, even if the personnel entitled to them are wearing dress coats [*mundiry*] (40).

24 October 1845 - The **Siberian Cadet Corps** is prescribed the following uniform:

a.) *For cadets and officers in the company, all field-grade officers, and the Director*—as for provincial corps with only the shoulder straps being different, being for this corps red with white piping and the yellow Cyrillic letters S. K.

b.) *For cadets and officers in the squadron*—as for the Orenburg-Nepluev Corps except that the base of the epaulettes and the girdles are red, while the shoulder straps on the everyday jackets and greatcoats are the same as in the company. The letters S. K. are on the epaulettes (Illus. 919) (41).

By **1 January 1846**, after all the changes set forth here, the **shoulder straps** of the various cadet corps were as follows:

a.) In the corps of the St.-Petersburg Military Educational Region [*Voenno-Uchebnyi Okrug*]:

   1st Cadet Corps - red with the number and letter 1. K.

   2nd Cadet Corps - white with the number and letter 2. K.

   Paul Cadet Corps - light blue with the letters P. K.

   Novgorod Graf Arakcheev Cadet Corps - dark green with red piping and the letters G. A.

   Finland Cadet Corps - light blue with the letters F. K.

   Nobiliary Regiment - yellow with no letters.

b.) In the corps of the Moscow Military Educational Region:

   1st Moscow Cadet Corps - red with white piping and the number and letter 1. M.

   2nd Moscow Cadet Corps - white with red piping and the number and letter 2. M.

   Orel-Bakhtin Cadet Corps - light blue with white piping and the letters O. B.

   Tula-Alexander Cadet Corps - light blue with white piping and the letters T. A.

   Michael-Voronezh Cadet Corps - dark green with white piping and the letters M. B.

   Tambov Cadet Corps - dark green with white piping and the letters T. K.

   Siberian Cadet Corps company - red with white piping and the letters S. K.

c.) In the corps of the Western Military Educational Region:

Polotsk Cadet Corps - red with light-blue piping and the letters P. K.

Peter-Poltava Cadet Corps - white with light-blue piping and the letters P. P.

Alexander-Brest Cadet Corps - light blue with red piping and the letters A. B.

All numbers and letters on the shoulder straps are yellow. On the gold field of officers' epaulettes the numbers and letters are embroidered in silver.

As for the *Orenburg-Nepluev Cadet Corps* and the *Siberian Corps' squadron*, both in the Moscow Military Educational Region, the scaled epaulettes are red copper, with a light-blue lining and the white metal letters O. N. prescribed for the former and red lining and the letters S. K. for the latter. Officers have silver letters fixed onto gold scaled epaulettes (42).

8 February 1846 - Pupils who have only just entered the **Alexander Cadet Corps** or the Young Boys' Section [*Maloletnoe otdelenie*] of the **1st Moscow Cadet Corps** are directed to keep only the single top button on their **jackets** (Illus. 920) until such time as they become fully acquainted with the corps regimen (43).

11 April 1847 - Having a uniform corresponding to the cossack style, officers of the **Orenburg-Neplyuev Cadet Corps** are directed to use a ***chekmen* coat** with the prescribed trim in place of the former jacket [*kurtka*] (Illus. 921) (44).

7 July 1847 – Particulars for **forage caps** for pupils of military educational institutions are confirmed as follows:

Finland Corps—dark-green forage cap, red cap band, red piping.

The **Alexander Young Boys' Corps** has dark-green forage caps with visors; red cap band without piping for the first three companies and the replacement section [*zapasnoe otdelenie*], while the 4th Company's is dark green with white piping on top. Cut-out letters on yellow cloth are A. K. for all companies, and piping around the top is red for the 1st Company, white for the 2nd, dark blue for the 3rd, and white for the 4th.

The **Nobiliary Regiment** has a dark-green forage cap and a red cap band without piping but with cut-out numbers and Cyrillic letters on yellow cloth: 1. G. R. and 2. G. R. for the Grenadier companies, and 1. R., etc., for the Musketeer companies. Piping around the top is red for the 1st Battalion and white for the 2nd (45).

11 December 1847 – **Firing-cap pouches** are to be worn on the crossbelts (46).

23 November 1849 - New **helmets** are to be made, in all three sizes [*vsekh trekh razryadov*], 1/4 vershok [7/8 inch] wider than before so that the come to the upper part of the ears (47).

9 March 1851 - Officers' epaulettes and pupils' shoulder straps in the **Peter-Poltava Cadet Corps** are to have the **monogram** designed by Peter the Great himself and preserved in the Imperial St.-Petersburg Academy of Sciences, consisting of the crossed Latin letters P. P. under a crown (Illus. 922) (48).

7 January 1852 - The **Highest Directive** announced in the Minister of War's Order No. 134 dated 13 December 1851 concerning the confirmation of new patterns of infantry drums, the method of fitting and attaching the water flask to the knapsack, the black strap for the greatcoat, the swordbelt and crossbelt, and the case or cover for the firing-nipple of percussion weapons, is to be in effect for Military Educational Institutions (49).

14 April 1853 - The **greatcoat shoulder straps** of pupils in Military Educational Institutions, lance-corporals, senior and junior non-commissioned officers, and sergeants are to have the same distinctions as are on the shoulder straps of dress coats and jackets, as is the case for other troops (50).

8 June 1853 - The following changes in the uniforms for pupils in Military Educational Institutions are confirmed:

1.) **Forage caps** are to made with a leather lining and a crown that is 1-3/8 vershoks [2-3/8 inches] high.

2.) **Deerskin gloves** for pupils are to be plain without any decoration (51).

B.) Conductor Company of the Main Engineering School
[Konduktorskaya rota Glavnago Inzhenernago uchilishcha].

11 February 1826 – Instead of their former dark-green pants (with high boots for officers and gaiters for others), officers and conductors [*konduktory*, i.e. engineer cadets - M. C.] are to wear long dark-green **pants** with red piping. Generals, field-grade officers, and adjutants are to have boots with the **spurs** driven in. All this is as prescribed at this time for these same ranks in the varioius cadet corps (Illus. 923) (52).

10 May 1826 - When mounted and in formation during the summer, generals, field-grade officers, and adjutants are to wear the same white linen **pants** as prescribed at this time for these same ranks in the several cadet corps (53).

11 January 1827 - For distinguishing **ranks**, officers' epaulettes are to have small forged or stamped gold stars according to the scheme established at this time fo officer' epaulettes in all arms and described in detail above for Grenadier regiments (54).

24 April 1828 - Officers and conductors are given new **shakos** of the same pattern as those introduced at this time in the cadet corps but, as before, with a white shako plate with the previous design in the half-circle (Illus. 924) (55).

26 December 1829 - Officers and conductors are to have uniform **buttons** with the same design as prescribed at this time for the buttons of the Life-Guards Sapper Battalion (56).

20 July 1830 - Conductors are ordered to have short swords of the pattern used in the Life-Guards Sapper Battalion (57).

20 August 1830 - Officers' rapiers are replaced with **half-sabers** with black scabbards and gilded brass mountings, as established at this same time for Army infantry troops (58).

16 December 1831 - In order that conductors may be distinguished among themselves according to **rank**, it is directed that silver lace be sewn onto the shoulder straps of coats and jackets as follows: for sergeants [*fel'dfebeli*]—all around and down the middle; for senior non-commissioned officers [*starshie unter-ofitsery*]—all around; for junior non-commissioned officers [*mladshie unter-ofitsery*]—down the middle; and for lance-corporals [*yefreitory*]—across, near the lower edge (59).

8 June 1832 - Officers are allowed to wear **moustaches** (60).

3 January 1833 - Cloth **half-gaiters** [*polushtiblety*] are abolished for officers and conductors. Additionally, **sword knots** are abolished for conductors except for those who have silver ones (61).

20 February 1833 - The white summer **pants** with buttons and integral spats are abolished for officers and conductors, being replaced by trousers without buttons or integral spats (Illus. 925) (62).

26 September 1834 - When going into and breaking camp during the summer, conductors, who since 1826 have shako covers and knapsacks as the infantry, are to likewise wear the **knapsack** on two straps crossing over the chest and not on two shoulder straps and one horizontal chest-strap (63).

20 August 1835 - When in camp, officers are to wear the **knapsack** in the same way as officers in all infantry units, using only two straps over the shoulders. The former horizontal strap, or chest strap, is abolished (64).

21 October 1836 - The girths on officers' **saddles** are to be dark-green with red stripes. In this same year officers' shabracks are given silver stars as in the Guards (65).

15 July 1837 - Officers' are given a new pattern **sash**, identical with that introduced at this time for all arms and described above in detail for Grenadier regiments (66).

17 December 1837 - Officers are given a new pattern of **epaulettes** with the addition of a fourth twist of thin cord (67).

2 January 1844 - Officers are to have an oval metallic **cockade** on the cap band of the forage cap, of the same colors as the cockades on officers' hats (68).

9 May 1844 - Officers and conductors are issued **helmets** instead of shakos, but keeping the shako plate as before and being in all details similar to the helmets received at this time by combatant ranks in the infantry (Illus. 926) (69).

4 January 1845 - Officers' **helmets** are to have a metal cockade on the right side under the chinscales, as established at this time throughout the Army (70).

9 August 1845 - When in camp dress, **helmets** are to be worn without plumes even when personnel entitled to plumes are wearing dress coats (71).

Changes relating to uniforms for conductors are also effective for **drummers**, who are distinguished from them by lace sewn onto the coat and a red helmet plume, as in the various Cadet corps.

7 July 1847 - The description of the **forage cap** for conductors is confirmed: dark-green cap, black band with red piping on both edges, red piping around the top (45).

14 April 1853 - Lance-corporals, senior and junior non-commissioned officers, and sergeants are to have the same insignia on **greatcoat shoulder straps** as on the dress coat and jacket (50).

C.) Artillery School [Artilleriiskoe uchilishcha].

11 February 1826 – In place of their former dark-green **pants** (with high boots for officers and knee-gaiters for others), officers and cadets [*yunkery*] are to wear long dark-green pants with red piping, while generals, field-grade officers, and adjutants are to have boots with the **spurs** driven in. All this is as introduced at this time in the various cadet corps and the Main Engineering School (Illus. 927) (72).

10 May 1826 – During summer when generals, field-grade officers, and adjutants are in formation and must be mounted, they are to wear the same white linen **pants** prescribed at this time for these ranks in the varioius cadet corps (73).

11 January 1827 – In order to distinguish **ranks**, officers' epaulettes are to have small forged silver stars according to the scheme established at this time for officers' epaulettes in all branches and described above in detail for Grenadier regiments (74).

24 April 1828 – Officers, cadets, and combatant lower ranks are given a new **shako** of the same pattern established at this time for cadet corps and the Nobiliary Regiment, keeping the design on the half-circle of the plate the same as before (Illus. 928) (75).

26 December 1829 – Officers and cadets are to have uniform **buttons** with the same design as prescribed at this time for Guards Foot and Horse Artillery (76).

20 August 1830 – Officers' rapiers are replaced with **half-sabers** with black scabbards and gilt brass mountings, as established at this time for the Army infantry (77).

16 December 1831 – In order that **ranks** may be distinguished among cadets, the shoulder straps of coats and jackets are to have gold lace sewn on in the same manner as described above in detail for the cadet corps (78).

8 June 1832 – Officers are allowed to have **moustaches** (79).

3 January 1833 – Cloth **half-gaiters** are abolished for officers and cadets. **Cartridge pouches** and **sword knots** are abolished for cadets, except for those who have knots in silver (80).

20 February 1833 – The summer **pants** with buttons and integral spats are abolished for officers and cadets, being replaced by trousers without buttons or integral spats (Illus. 929) (81).

29 May 1834 – Under no circumstances are officers to have **knapsacks** when in formation, which previously they wore just as officers in other branches, and at all times they are to wear **spurs** and straps on the pants under the sole (82).

26 September 1834 – When moving during summer into and out of camp, cadets, who since 1826 have had shako covers and knapsacks as in the infantry, are to likewise wear the **knapsack** using two crossbelts and not two shoulder belts and a chest strap (83).

21 October 1836 – The girths of officers' **saddles** are to be dark green with red stripes, and henceforth officers' shabracks are to have silver stars as in the Guards (84).

15 July 1837 – Officers are given a new-pattern **sash** identical to that introduced at this time in all branches and described in detail above for Grenadier regiments (85).

17 December 1837 – Officers are given a new-pattern **epaulette** with an additional fourth twist of cord (86).

2 January 1844 – The cap bands of officers' **forage caps** are to have an elongated metal cockade in the same colors as prescribed for the cockade on officers' hats (87).

9 May 1844 – In place of shakos, officers and cadets are given **helmets** with the former shako plate. These are in every way like the helmets received at this time by combat ranks in the infantry (Illus. 930) (88).

4 January 1845 – Officers are to have a metallic **cockade** on the right side of the helmet under the chinscales, just as established at this time for other troops (Illus. 931) (89).

9 August 1845 – When in camp dress, **helmets** are to be worn without plumes even though personnel entitled to them are wearing their dress coats (90).

Changes relating to uniforms for cadets are also effective for **drummers**, distinguished by coats with sewn-on lace just as in Cadet corps, and by red plumes on their helmets.

7 July 1847 – For cadets of the Artillery School the **forage cap** is confirmed as dark green with a black band edged on both sides with red piping, along with red piping around the crown (45).

20 September 1849 – In memory of its famours Founder, the Artillery School is henceforth ordered to be called the **Michael Artillery School** [*Mikhailvoskoe Artilleriiskoe uchilishche*]. Its officers' epaulettes and its pupils' shoulder straps are to have a **monogram** formed by an M under a crown (Illus. 932) (91).

8 June 1853 – For the Michael Artillery School a **thin light of color** is allowed to show between the lace and piping on the dress coat (51).

D.) HIS IMPERIAL MAJESTY'S *Corps of Pages.*
[Pazheskii EGO IMPERATORSKAGO VELICHESTVA korpus.]

Based on the general changes of 11 February 1826 in the uniforms of personnel in Military Educational Institutions and in the table of 24 February 1827 for items of uniform, equipment, armament, and so on for the **Corps of Pages**, orders of dress are as follows:

1.) *Chamber-pages in ceremonial uniform [Kamer-pazhi v prazdnichnoi forme]* (for duty at HIGHEST Court on those days when the guard mount is to the be normal uniform, and when on leave)—single-breasted dark-green coat with red collar, cuffs, shoulder straps, and piping (down the front and from the front to the turnbacks, and on the turnbacks), gold lace trim, or buttonholes, on the collar, sleeves, and skirts, gold lace around the shoulder straps, and gilt buttons; dark-green trousers with red piping; boots with driven-in spurs; suede gloves; three-cornered officer's hat and an officer's cavalry rapier [*shpaga*] without a sword knot (Illus. 933).

2.) *Chamber-pages in parade dress [paradnaya forma]* (for duty at HIGHEST Court on those days when the guard mount is to be with sashes or in parade uniform)—as the previous order of dress but with white cloth pants and half-boots [*botforty*] with attached spurs instead of trousers and boots with driven-in spurs (Illus. 933).

3.) *Chamber-pages likewise in parade dress* (when attending the IMPERIAL Family on horseback)—all as for the previous order of dress but with pants of deerskin instead of cloth.

4.) *Chamber-pages*—for morning duty at HIGHEST Court when outside the city and also for duty at the Corps and when riding on horseback—as for parade dress but in place of the dress coat, an undress coat [*vitse-mundir*] of the same colors and cut without embroidery or lace, without shoulder straps, with dark-green cuffs and pocket flaps, both with red piping, and with buttons covered with black silk (Illus. 934).

5.) *Pages in ceremonial uniform* (when granted home leave)—as for court-pages but without the sword; the coat is without red piping or gold lace on the skirts, and the boots do not have spurs (Illus. 935).

6.) *Pages in parade dress* (for details to HIGHEST Court and HIGHEST appearances in general)—as for ceremonial uniform but white cloth pants tied at the knee instead of dark-green trousers and boots; stockings and shoes with gilt buckles (Illus. 935).

7.) *Chamber-pages in formation uniform [stroevaya forma]*—as for ceremonial dress but without gloves; in winter with the addition of black cloth half-gaiters while in summer with the addition of white linen gaiters; boots without spurs; shako instead of hat, with the cadet shako plate, non-commissioned officer's lower pompon and white upper pompon; accouterments and weapons as prescribed for cadets, with a silver sword knot on the shortsword (Illus. 936).

8.) *Pages in formation uniform*—as for ceremonial dress but without gloves; in winter with black cloth half-gaiters and in summer with linen gaiters; shoe as for court-pages instead of the hat, but with a white lower pompon with a black center; cadet arms and accouterments (Illus. 936).

9.) *Chamber-pages and pages in field formation uniform [pokhodnaya stroevaya forma]*—all as in the preceding but instead of the dress coat a grey cadet greatcoat with red collar and shoulder straps; shako and pouch in black; oilskin covers with the Cyrillic letters P. R. [*Pazheskaya rota* = page company]; shortsword without sword knot (Illus. 937).

10.) *Chamber-pages and pages in everyday, or classroom, dress [vsednevnaya ili klassnaya forma]*—single-breasted dark-green jacket [*kurtka*] with similarly colored slit cuffs, red collar piped dark green, dark-green shoulder straps piped red, and brass buttons; dark-green cloth trousers with red piping, but in summer grey nankeen trousers; dark-green forage cap with a red band and red piping around the top of the crown; boots without spurs (Illus. 937).

Besides formation uniforms, chamber-pages as well as pages retain dark-green officer-pattern greatcoats with a red collar and the same buttons as on the dress coat.

Officers of the Corps of Pages are prescribed the same uniform clothing as officers of Cadet corps in the capital cities, but with their previous embroidery and red base to the epaulettes and small cross-straps on the shoulder. For formation uniform they are given shakos with the same cadet plate as for chamber-pages and pages, but gilded (Illus. 938) (92).

24 April 1828 – Officers, chamber-pages, and pages in formation uniform are given new **shakos** of the same pattern as received at this time by officers and pupils in the various Cadet corps (Illus. 939) (93).

16 December 1829 – Instead of red cuffs on the **frock coat**, officers are to have dark-green cuffs with red piping (94).

26 December 1829 – Officers, chamber-pages, and pages are to have **buttons** with an image of the Sovereign's coat-of-arms, as prescribed at this time for the uniforms of the several Cadet corps (95).

20 August 1830 – Officers' rapiers are replaced with **half-sabers** like those received at this time by officers of the various Cadet corps (96).

8 June 1832 – Officers are allowed to have **moustaches** (97).

30 July 1832 – Chamber-pages and pages are directed to have red piping on the cuffs of the **jacket** and dark-green piping on the shoulder straps of the formation **greatcoat** (98).

3 January 1833 – Cloth **half-gaiters** are abolished for officers, chamber-pages, and pages. Pages' sword knots on the shortswords are also removed (99).

20 February 1833 – For officers, chamber-pages, and pages the summer formation **pants** with buttons and integral spats are replaced by trousers without buttons or spats (Illus. 940) (100).

26 September 1834 – Chamber-pages and pages, who have had shako covers and knapsacks as for infantry troops, are to also wear the **knapsack** on two crossbelts and not on two shoulder belts and a chest strap (101).

20 August 1835 – When in camp, officers are to wear the **knapsack** in the manner of the officers of all other branches, on only two shoulder belts, while the previous cross-strap, or chest strap, is abolished. (102).

15 July 1837 – Officers are given a new-pattern **sash** identical to that introduced at this time in all branches and described in detail above for Grenadier regiments (103).

17 December 1837 – Officers are given a new-pattern **epaulette** with an additional fourth twist of thin cord (104).

2 January 1844 – Officers are to have an elongated metal **cockade** on the band of the forage cap, in the same colors as prescribed for the cockade on officers' hats (105).

9 May 1844 – Instead of shakos, officers, chamber-pages, and pages are given **helmets** with the existing shako plate and in every way similar to the helmets received at this time by the variouis Cadet corps (Illus. 941) (106).

7 December 1844 – **Generals** of the Corps of Pages, when wearing the coat prescribed for this body off duty, are to have a white **plume** on the hat instead of black (107).

4 January 1845 – Officers' helmets are to have a metallic **cockade** on the right side of the helmet under the chinscales, as established at this time throughout the Army (108).

9 August 1845 – When in camp dress, **helmets** are to be worn without plumes, even if personnel entitled to them are in their dress coats (109).

The changes in the formation dress of chamber-pages and pages also apply to **drummers**, who have the same lace on their coats as in the several Cadet corps.

7 July 1847 – The pattern of **forage cap** for pupils in the Corps of Pages is confirmed as: dark-green forage cap, red band, red piping around the top (45).

16 November 1852 – It is ordered that:

1.) Pupils in the Corps of Pages have a new pattern **helmet** in place of hats, with a white plume for chamber-pages, a black one for pages (Illus. 942), and for pages not assigned to the Corps—no plume. These helmets are to used in all those situations in which up to now hats have been worn, while helmets worn in troop formation [*frontovyya kaski*] are to be kept as before, for formation dress.

2.) While on duty at HIGHEST Court, pages are to wear white **pants** and **boots** in place of breeches [*shtany*] with stockings and shoes (Illus. 943) (110).

E.) School for Guards Officer-Candidates and Cadets.
[Shkola Gvardeiskikh Podpraporshchikov i Yunkerov.]

Up to the following new Directive from 1838 for the **School for Guards Officer-Candidates and Cadets**, its officers, officer-candidates, and cadets had the uniforms, weapons, and horse furniture prescribed for those regiments and other troop units to which they belonged.

8 October 1838 – All combatant field and company-grade officers of the School, as well as of officer-candidates [*podpraporshchiki*, or sub-ensigns] in the foot company and cadets [*yunkera*, or junkers] in the mounted squadron, are prescribed uniforms as follows: in the company—as for the **Life-Guards Moscow Regiment**, and in the squadron—as for the **Life-Guards Horse-Grenadier Regiment**, with the addition of a gold edge to officers' collars, sleeves, and cuff flaps, the replacement of buttonholes of tape [*bason*] on the dress coats of officer-candidates and cadets with gold ones of galloon, and the exchange in the squadron of the horse-grenadier helmet for a guards cavalry shako with yellow cords and pompon (Illus. 944 and 945). (Note: uniforms, arms, and horse equipment for the Life-Guards Moscow and Horse-Grenadier Regiments are described above in Chapter XXIII.) Horse are to be bays [*gnedoi*]. For classroom, or everyday, dress, officer-candidates are prescribed the same jacket as for the several Cadet corps (with red shoulder straps without any letters) and the same trousers and forages caps (with red bands and edging), while cadets have grey-blue cloth riding trousers with red piping and leather reinforcement instead of pants. Officer-candidates are given dark-grey greatcoats with red collar and shoulder straps, dark-green tabs on the collar, and brass buttons, while cadets additionally have dark-green piping on the edges of the collar (112).

3 December 1838 – Cadets in the squadron are to have **epaulettes** without fringes, as in the Life-Guards Lancer Regiment (Illus. 946)(113).

23 April 1839 – These same cadets are to have **dragoon muskets** when in foot formation but when mounted—**carbines** and **lances** with red shafts and pennants whose two parts next to the shaft are white while the stripe between them as well as the ends are red (Illus. 946) (114).

2 January 1844 – Officers' forage caps in the company and squadron are to have an elongated metallic **cockade** on the band in the same colors as prescribed for the cockade on officers' hats (115).

9 May 1844 – In place of shakos, field and company-grade officers, officer-candidates, and cadets are given **helmets** with black hair plumes, like those introduced at this time in the Guards infantry and cavalry. In the squadron there is a brass edge to the front peak but in the company—no edge (Illus. 947) (116).

7 December 1844 – When wearing the company coat [*rotnyi mundir*], the **Commander of the School**, if he is of general-officer rank, is to have a white plume on his hat instead of black (117).

4 January 1845 – Officers are to have a metal **cockade** on the right side of the helmet under the chinscales, as laid down at this time for the Army as a whole (Illus. 948) (118).

9 August 1845 – When in camp dress [*lagernaya forma*], **helmets** are to be worn without plume even though personnel entitled to them may be wearing dress coats (119).

The uniform changes mentioned here also applied to **drummers** and **hornists** in the company and **drummers** and **trumpeters** in the squadron, who have a coat, accouterments, and weapons like those of these same ranks in the Life-Guards Moscow and Horse-Grenadier Regiments with the changes as prescribed for the School (120).

LIV. GENERAL OFFICERS. [*Generalitet voobshche.*]

11 February 1826 – On the special days of the official calendar and during grand reviews, generals are to wear, as before, **dress coats** [*mundiry*] with gold embroidery (on dark-green cloth for garrison generals and on red for all others), white pants with high boots and buckled-on spurs. On all other occasions, when in the **undress coat** [*vitse-mundir*] or frock coat [*syurtuk*], long dark-green pants are worn over short boots with driven-in spurs. For infantry generals these pants are prescribed to have red piping (Illus. 949) except in the Separate Lithuanian Corps where the piping is raspberry. Cavalry generals have red stripes and piping on the pants, or raspberry in the Lithuanian Corps (Illus. 950). Garrison generals' pants have no piping (Illus. 951). Along with these changes, on the parade coats [*paradnye mundiry*] of infantry and cavalry generals the dark-green cuffs flaps are replaced by red (Illus. 949). Cavalry generals keep the grey riding trousers with red stripes and piping, or raspberry in the Lithuanian Corps (121).

10 June 1826 – Infantry generals are forbidden to wear the **grey riding trousers** with colored stripes, in use since 1814, but cavalry generals are allowed to wear them with the undress coat with only a single line of red piping (raspberry in the Lithuanian Corps) on the side seams and no stripe (122).

1 January 1827 - On the embroidered coat [*shitye mundiry*] as well as on the undress coat and frock coat, generals are to have small stamped and forged silver **stars** on gold epaulettes and gold ones on silver epaulettes, as follows: for Major-Generals—two; for Lieutenant-Generals—three. The stars are of the same appearance and arrangement as described in detail for Grenadier regiments. Epaulettes of Generals of Infantry, of Cavalry, and of Artillery, and of Engineer-Generals do not have these stars, and General-Field Marshals' epaulettes are to have two crossed batons (Illus. 953) (123).

19 May 1829 – When wearing the sash and embroidered coat, generals of heavy cavalry are to carry the **broadsword** [*palash*] instead of the rapier [*shpaga*], on a gold swordbelt in the manner established for generals of light cavalry (Illus. 954). In the same manner the sword is also to be worn with the undress coat whenever in formation. But when not in formation and without the sash, generals are to have the rapier as before (124).

9 July 1829 – As a clarification of the 11 February and 10 June 1826 regulations changing the uniform, it is ordered that in general all cavalry general officers shall have **white pants** when wearing the embroidered parade coat, **dark-green pants** with red stripes and piping when wearing the undress coat, and **grey riding trousers** without stripes but with piping when on campaign. Cavalry generals in the Guards cavalry stationed in Warsaw and in the Lithuanian Lancer Division are to have raspberry piping, instead of red, on both the dark-green pants and grey riding trousers, with no stripes (125).

29 December 1829 – The **buttons** on generals' embroidered coats and undress coats, as well as on frock coats and greatcoats, are to have an image of a two-headed eagle as on the buttons confirmed at this time for the Guards (126).

25 November 1830 – Cavalry generals and generals assigned to the cavalry are to have their **dark-green pants** without stripes, with a single line of red piping (Illus. 955) (127).

9 May 1831 – With the elimination of all the exceptions to general uniform regulations that existed for the former Separate Lithuanian Corps, the color for **stripes and piping** on the uniforms for generals in the Russian Army can no longer be raspberry (128).

1 January 1832 – Generals who have **gold rapiers or sabers** decorated with diamonds and inscribed *"For Courage"* are to have these without sword knots (129).

8 June 1832 – All generals are allowed to wear **moustaches** (130).

16

26 February 1836 – Generals of heavy cavalry are to have **saddles** like those prescribed for officers of this branch, with bearskin [*medvedzhii*] **shabracks**, also as for officers (131).

15 July 1837 – Generals are given a new-pattern **sash** with a narrow silver lace band instead of the previous wide one, with three stripes of light-orange and black silk. The sash is worn with its entire unfolded width fitting between the two lowest buttons of the coat (132) .

17 December 1837 – Generals are given **epaulettes** of a new pattern with an additional fourth thin twist of cord (133).

23 January 1841 – The capes on generals' **greatcoats** are to be 1 arshin [28 inches] long as measured from the lower end of the collar (134).

8 April 1843 – Generals in the Internal Guard [*Vnutrennyaya Strazha*] are to have **dress and undress coats** with red collars and cuffs instead of dark green, so as to be like generals in the Army (135).

Together with this, the standard general officer's **shabrack**, **pistol holder**, and **saddlecloth** are to have a silver eight-pointed St.-Andrew's star, with the inscription around eagle *"For Faith and Fidelity" ["Za Vera i Vernost'"]*. These shabracks and saddlecloths are to be of the following pattern:

a.) For infantry generals and generals in the Guards Cuirassier Division—shabracks [*chepraki*], 13-1/2 vershoks [23-1/2 inches] long on top from the withers to the croup, 16-7/8 [29-1/2] below, 10 [17-1/2] wide in front, 11-1/2 [20-1/8] wide at the back along the slanted edge; the *holster* is 5-1/2 vershoks [9-5/8 inches] long. The stars sewn on the rear corners of the shabrack are to be 3 vershoks [5-1/4 inches] in size while those on the holsters are 2-1/2 [4-3/8] (Illus. 956). The surcingle [*trok*] of infantry generals' shabracks has dark-green and red stripes, while for generals in the Guards Cuirassier Division the stripes are red and white

b.) For army Cuirassier generals—saddlecloths [*val'trapy*] with rounded front corners with 2-1/2 vershok [4-3/8 inch] stars and pointed rear corners with 3-vershok [5-1/4 inch] stars (Illus. 957). The surcingle is lined with dark-green cloth.

c.) For light-cavalry generals except Hussars—saddlecloths as above except that the rear corners are rounded like the front ones instead ov being pointed.

d.) For Hussar generals—saddlecloths of hussar pattern with the same stars and surcingle as for the saddlecloths above (136).

2 January 1844 – The cap band of general officers' forage caps is to have a **cockade** in front as established at this same time for all branches and described above for the uniform for Grenadier regiments (137)

13 August 1845 – Generals wearing the standard army undress coat or frock coat are allowed to wear **helmets** of the pattern established on 9 May 1844 and 4 January 1845 for generals and field and company-grade offices of troop formations, but with ornate [*uzorchatye*] gilt mountings instead of being plain (Illus. 958). In the Guards the helmet has the Guards plate and in the Army its own plate, with a silver Imperial crown affixed to the center of the shield (Illus. 958, 959, and 960). Both these helmets, Guards and Army, have an embossed image of an Imperial crown on the attachment points of the chinscales and of the same color as the scales. When worn with the undress coat, both helmets have a white horsehair plume (138).

6 October 1845 – The following instructions are confirmed by HIGHEST Authority as supplement to the above directive regarding generals' **helmets**:

1.) Generals who are in the Guards Corps by virtue of being commanders of actual Guards units or who are enrolled in Guards divisions although they are not on the rolls of any Guards regiment, are to wear the helmet with the eagle as confirmed for Guards regiments when in the standard Army undress coat or frock coat.

2.) Generals who are in the Guards Corps as commanders of units which do not actually belong to the Guard are to wear the helmet with the Army helmet plate when in the standard Army undress coat or frock.

3.) Generals commanding Army units but who are on the rolls of a Guards regiment are also to wear the helmet with the Army plate when in the undress coat or frock (139).

9 January 1848 - On those days when after the mounting of the guard they must remain in ceremonial dress [*prazdnichnaya forma*], generals without a regimental uniform are allowed to wear, when walking out, **frock coats** with winter pants and **helmets** with plumes or—if they are authorized to have them—hats (140).

21 September 1849 - When on duty and in formation, generals are ordered to no longer wear the hat, but to be in **helmets**. When not on duty, however, they are allowed as before to use the **hat** if they wish (141).

27 September 1849 - Generals in the War Ministry [*Voennoe Ministerstvo*] are to wear **helmets** instead of hats, of the pattern confirmed for field and company-grade officers of the Ministry but with a gold Imperial crown on the shield of the helmet plate, similar to standard Army generals' helmets and with a white hair plume (142).

13 October 1849 - Generals of the Infantry, Foot Artillery, General Staff, and Engineers who are assigned to the War

Ministry are to wear infantry **half-sabers** instead of rapiers when in the undress coat, but are to have the **rapier** as before when in the standard general officer's coat. However, generals of the heavy cavalry are to have cavalry **rapiers** when in the undress coat and **broadswords**, as before, when in the standard coat (143).

15 February 1850 - All military generals in the **Caucasus** who do not belong to troop formations are to have a uniform like that confirmed for troops of the Separate Caucasus Corps, in accordance with the following description:

Shapka headdress (in place of the helmet and hat) like that confirmed for troops of the Caucasus Corps. The top of the headdress is of red cloth and when worn with the standard general's parade half-caftan [paradnyi polukaftan] has gold general officer's embroidery along the four seams and lower edge, but when worn with the standard general officer's undress half-caftan [vitse-polukaftan] it has gold lace with two narrow red stripes down the center.

Half-caftan (in place of the coat and frock). Cut exactly as confirmed for troops of the Caucasus Corps and with buttons of the same stamp and color as the previous coat. Nine buttons are on the front while four buttons are in the back at the waist and on the pocket flaps. The lining of the half-caftan is black stamin for all. The standard general's parade half-caftan has a collar and cuffs with flaps as presently on the parade coat. The cuff flaps themselves have embroidery of the pattern for cossack generals' half-caftans. There is red piping on the front along the buttons and down the skirt to the lower edge of the half-caftan (Illus. 961).

The *standard general's undress half-caftan* [obshche-general'skii vitse-polukaftan] has a red cloth collar closed with little hooks. The cuffs are dark green without flaps, with red cloth piping along the top edge. The pocket flaps have red piping (Illus. 962). *Note: Generals in the Artillery and Corps of Engineers have this half-caftan with a black collar with red piping around it, while the cuffs are of black cloth with red piping also.*

Sharavary trousers—of the pattern confirmed for troops of the Separate Caucasus Corps in place of pants—of dark-green cloth with red piping, but in place of riding trousers—of grey-blue cloth with red piping.

Arms—In place of the broadsword, rapier, saber, and half-saber—a dragoon-pattern saber on the swordbelt prescribed for that. The lace and fittings on the swordbelt are gilt and the lining is black morocco. The sword knot for the saber is of cavalry pattern for cavalry generals and of infantry pattern for those in the infantry (144).

18 February 1854 – Generals are to have the **horse furniture** established on 15 November 1853. This is of the Guards Cuirassier pattern for those the Guards Cuirassier Division while those in the entire rest of the cavalry as well as in the Horse Artillery and Horse Pioneers have the Light Cavalry pattern (see Army Cuirassier regiments) (145).

29 April 1854 - In wartime generals are to have campaign greatcoats like those established at this time for Army and Guards troops, with red collars and shoulder straps (146).

LV. GENERAL-ADJUTANTS and AIDES-DE-CAMP. [*General-Ad"yutanty i Fligel-Ad"yutanty.*]

14 and 15 December 1825 – The General-Adjutants and Aides-de-Camp appointed to HIS IMPERIAL MAJESTY on these dates are to have a representation on their epaulettes of the personal **cipher** of the SOVEREIGN EMPEROR NICHOLAS PAVLOVICH, in gold on silver epaulettes and in silver on gold ones (Illus. 963). This also applies for persons subsequently named to these appointments while those already previously holding such positions are to keep the cipher of EMPEROR ALEXANDER I (147).

11 February 1826 – On the scheduled feast days of the official calendar and at grand reviews General-Adjutants are to wear, as before, **white pants** and **high boots** with buckled-on spurs. In all other situations with any uniform they, as well as Aides-de-Camp, are to wear **dark-green pants** and **short boots** with driven-in spurs. Generals and Aides-de-Camp of the infantry are prescribed these pants with red piping while in the cavalry they additionally have red stripes (Illus. 964 and 965) (148).

10 June 1826 – Aides-de-Camp are to wear, as before, **white pants** and **high boots** with buckled spurs in all situations where it is laid down that these are to be worn by Generals (149).

1 January 1828 – General-Adjutants and Aides-de-Camp, in addition to the HIGHEST, cipher, are to have small **stars** on the epaulettes to distinguish **rank** (in silver for gold epaulettes and in gold when on silver), according to the same rules as described in detail above for Grenadier regiments and the uniform for general officers (150).

In 1828 – General-Adjutants and Aides-de-Camp are given **campaign saddlecloths** in addition to their prescribed shabracks with holsters and housings, of black fleece with the exact same stars as on the parade shabrack and housings (in gold for General-Adjutants and silver for Aides-de-Camp), with 1 vershok [1-3/4 inch] wide red cloth trim along the edges, lined on the outside with gold or silver cord (according to the color of the stars) (Illus. 966) (151).

29 December 1829 – General-Adjutants and Aides-de-Camp are to have uniform **buttons** with the image of a two-headed eagle, like the buttons confirmed at this time for the Guards (152).

25 November 1830 – General-Adjutants and Aides-de-Camp of the Cavalry are to have dark-green **pants** with only a single line of red piping and no stripes (153).

1 January 1832 – General-Adjutants who have a **gold sword** or **saber** decorated with diamonds and inscribed *"For Courage"* are to wear these without sword knots (154).

8 June 1832 – All General-Adjutants and Aides-de-Camp may wear **moustaches** (155).

2 March 1834 - Aides-de-Camp who are part of or attached to regiments or other troop units are to wear the **uniform** prescribed for those regiments and units for as long as they are with them, at the same time keeping the HIGHEST cipher on epaulettes, and aiguilettes. This last item, as well as the epaulettes, is the same color as the buttons, while the cipher is silver when on gold epaulettes and gold when on silver ones (156).

29 May 1836 – Aides-de-Camp are to have **saddle girths** according to the arm of service to which they belong (157).

15 July 1837 – General-Adjutants and Aides-de-Camp are given a new-pattern **sash**, being a narrow silver lace band instead of a wide one as before, with three stripes of light-orange and black silk, and worn around the body so that its entire width is between the two bottom coat buttons (158).

17 December 1837 – General-Adjutants and Aides-de-Camp are given new-pattern **epauletts**, with an additional fourth thin twist of cord (159).

23 January 1841 – The capes on **greatcoats** of General-Adjutants and Aides-de-Camp are to be 1 arshin [28-inches] long as measured from the bottom edge of the collar (160).

18 April 1843 – When standing with troops and part of one of their formations, General-Adjutants and Aides-de-Camp are to wear the **hat** athwart [*pryamo*] and not fore-and-aft [*s polya*] (161).

2 January 1844 – General-Adjutants and Aides-de-Camp are to have a **cockade** on the front of the band of the forage cap, as laid down for all arms and described above in detail for the uniforms of Grenadier regiments (162).

1 December 1844 – Aides-de-Camp are to have **helmets** instead of hats, just like those introduced for line troops on 9 May of this year. They have silvered mountings and a Guards helmet plate, in the middle of which on the eagle's shield is the HIGHEST cipher in gold. The plume is of white horse hair (Illus. 967 and 968) (163).

4 January 1845 – On the right side of these helmets, under the chinscales, there is to be a metal **cockade** as laid down at this time for generals and field and company-grade officers of line troops (Illus. 969) (164).

6 October 1845 – When in the standard army undress coat or the frock coat, General-Adjutants are authorized to wear the **helmet** established on 13 August of this year for all general officers. For those enrolled in Guards regiments the helmet has the Guards plate, while for generals not so enrolled, the helmet plate is the army pattern for general officers (165).

2 May 1846 - It is directed that all General-Adjutants, when wearing the coat for that appointment, be allowed to wear the general officer's **helmet** with the Guards eagle (166).

6 June 1846 – When in the General-Adjutant's coat and white pants, General-Adjutants are to wear **hats**. Helmets, though, are to worn with the coat and green pants and with the frock coat (167).

18 July 1846 – General-Adjutants on the rolls of Guards units are prescribed **helmets** with the Guards eagle, just as General-Adjutants who are enrolled in the Guard (168).

9 January 1848 – On those days when ceremonial dress is prescribed after guard mount, General-Adjutants and Aides-de-Camp are allowed to wear **frock coats** with green pants when walking out, along with the helmet and plume, or the hat for those so authorized (169).

27 September 1849 – General-Adjutants and Aides-de-Camp on duty in the War Ministry are to wear **helmets** with the Guards plate when in the uniform of that Ministry (170).

13 October 1849 – Aides-de-Camp of the Infantry and Foot Artillery are to carry infantry **half-sabers** in place of rapiers, while those in the Heavy Cavalry are to have **broadswords** when wearing the sash and cavalry **rapiers** when not wearing the sash (171).

15 February 1850 – General-Adjutants and Aides-de-Camp in the **Caucasus** who are not part of any troop unit are to be uniformed according to the following description:
Shapka (in place of the helmet and hat) like that confirmed for troops of the Caucaus Corps. For General-Adjutants the top of the *shapka* headdress is of red cloth while for Aides-de-Camp it is dark green; for General-Adjutants wearing the parade half-caftan the top of the headdress has gold embroidery along the four seams and bottom edge, while when wearing the undress half-caftan it has gold lace with two thin red stripes down the center; for Aides-de-Camp the top of

the headdress has silver lace with two thin red stripes down the center.

Half-caftan [polukaftan]—cut similarly to that confirmed for troops of the Caucasus Corps, with the same buttons as on the previous dress coat: nine in front and four in back at the waist and on the pocket flaps; the half-caftan is lined with black stamin. The General-Adjutant's parade half-caftan has a collar and cuffs with flaps as were on the coat. There is white piping on the front alongside the buttons and down the skirt to the bottom edge of the half-caftan, and on the pocket flaps. The parade half-caftan for Aides-de-Camp is as for General-Adjutants except for embroidery and buttons, which remain the same as were on the coat (Illus. 970). The *undress half-caftan [vitse-polukaftan]* of General-Adjutants and Aides-de-Camp has a collar of red cloth, closed with small hooks, dark-green cuffs without flaps, white piping on the collar, down the front to the bottom of the skirt, around the cuffs, and on the pocket flaps, and buttons as prescribed by rank (Illus. 971).

Sharavary pants are of the pattern confirmed for troops of the Caucasus Corps, replacing the previous pants. They are of dark-green cloth with red piping, and when worn in place of riding trousers they are of dark grey-blue cloth with red piping.

The saber [*sablya*] is of dragoon pattern, on the swordbelt prescribed for that type. Lace and fittings for the swordbelt are in the color of the buttons—silver or gold; the swordbelt is lined with black morocco. The sword knot for the saber is the cavalry pattern for those in the cavalry and the infantry pattern for others (172).

7 February 1852 – It is directed:

1.) General-Adjutants and Aides-de-Camp in hussar uniform are to wear the **aiguilette** of the approved pattern on the dolman(if the pelisse is worn slung), on the pelisse (if it is worn arms in sleeves), on the jacket [*kurtka*], and on the Hungarian undress coat [*vengerka*].

2.) This aiguilette is to be in the same color as the braid and worn on the right shoulder.

3.) A stamped and forged monogram with a crown and boss [*pugovka*] is to be set on the shoulder knot of the aiguilette; the boss is like the one worn on the left shoulder to fasten the shoulder cord (Illus. 972).

4.) The shoulder knot is to be lined with gold or silver cloth according to the color of the braid (173).

29 April 1854 – In wartime General-Adjutants and Aides-de-Camp are to have campaign greatcoats (Illus. 973) as established for Guards troops (174).

LVI. GENERALS OF HIS IMPERIAL MAJESTY'S SUITE.
[*Generaly Svity EGO IMPERATORSKAGO VELICHESTVA.*]

29 June 1828 – Generals of HIS IMPERIAL MAJESTY'S Suite are to have the same **uniform** as Aides-de-Camp but without the aiguilette and with epaulettes without a cipher; plumes are according to branch of service: black for infantry and white for cavalry; horse furniture as for Aides-de-Camp (Illus. 974). They are also authorized the standard general officer's dress coat with gold emroidery and the general officer's undress coat without embroidery, in accordance with the existing and pertinent general rules (175).

29 December 1829 – Generals of HIS IMPERIAL MAJESTY'S Suite are to have uniform **buttons** with the image of a two-headed eagle, like the buttons approved at this time for the Guards (176).

1 January 1832 – Generals of HIS IMPERIAL MAJESTY'S Suite with a **gold sword** or **saber** decorated with diamonds and inscribed *"For Courage"* are to wear these without sword knots (177).

8 June 1832 – All Generals of HIS IMPERIAL MAJESTY'S Suite are authorized to wear **moustaches** (178).

29 May 1836 - Generals of HIS IMPERIAL MAJESTY'S Suite are to have saddle **girths** according to the arm of service to which they belong (179).

15 July 1837 – Generals of HIS IMPERIAL MAJESTY'S Suite are given a new-pattern **sash** with a narrow silver belt of silver lace instead of the previous wide one, with three stripes of light-orange and black silk, and wrapped around the body so that its entire width is between the two bottom coat buttons (180).

17 December 1837 – Generals of HIS IMPERIAL MAJESTY'S Suite are given **epauletts** of the new pattern with an additional fourth thin twist of cord (181).

23 January 1841 – The capes on the **greatcoats** of Generals of HIS IMPERIAL MAJESTY'S Suite are to be 1 arshin [28-inches] long as measured from the bottom edge of the collar (182).

18 April 1843 – When they are at the front of troops as part of one of their formations, Generals of HIS IMPERIAL MAJESTY'S Suite are to wear the **hat** athwart [*pryamo*] and not fore-and-aft [*s polya*] (183).

2 January 1844 – There is to be a **cockade** on the front of the forage cap band (184).

1 December 1844 – **Hats** with white plumes are to be worn when in the suite coat [*svitskii mundir*] (185).

4 July 1845 – **Helmets** as for Aides-de-Camp (Illus. 975) are to be worn with the suite coat while **hats** are to be worn with the general officer's coat, as before (186).

9 July 1846 – When in the standard army coat, Generals of HIS IMPERIAL MAJESTY'S Suite are authorized to wear general officers' **helmets** with the Guards eagle (187).

27 September 1849 - Those on duty in the War Ministry are to have **helmets** with a Guards plate (188).

13 October 1849 – Those in the Infantry or Foot Artillery are to carry **half-sabers** instead of rapiers, while those in the Heavy Cavalry are to carry **broadswords** when wearing the sash and cavalry **rapiers** when not wearing the sash (189).

15 February 1850 – Those in the **Caucasus** but not part of any troop unit are to be uniformed according to the following description:

Shapka headdress in the Caucasian style; of red cloth trimmed on the four seams and along the lower edge with silver lace with two narrow red stripes down the center.

Half-caftan [polukaftan], in the Caucasian style; its buttons are the same color and pattern as were on the coats, nine in front and four in back on the waist and pocket flaps. The lining is black stamin. The parade half-caftan has a collar and cuffs with flaps as on the previous coat. There is white piping in front along the buttons and down to the bottom edge of the half-caftan's skirt and on the pocket flaps (Illus. 976). The *undress half-caftan [vitse-polukaftan]* has a collar of red cloth closed with small hooks, dark-green cuffs without flaps, and white piping on the collar, down the front to the bottom of the skirt, around the cuffs, and on the pocket flaps.

Sharavary pants are of dark-green cloth with red piping when used in place of the previous pants, and when worn in place of riding trousers they are of dark grey-blue cloth with red piping.

The saber is of dragoon pattern, on the sword-belt made of silver lace and black morocco, with silver fittings. For those in the cavalry the sword knot is the cavalry pattern while for those in the infantry—the infantry pattern (190).

29 April 1854 – In wartime Generals of HIS IMPERIAL MAJESTY'S Suite are to have campaign greatcoats of the pattern established at this time for troops of the Guard and Army (191).

Russian Genrral of major staff 1848 around

NOTES

(1) *Collection of Laws and Regulations*, 1826, Book I, pg. 105.

(2) Ibid., Book II, pg. 11.

(3) Ibid., pg. 47.

(4) Ibid., 1827, Book I, pg. 3, and information received from the 1st and 2nd Cadet Corps and Nobiliary Regiment.

(5) *Complete Collection of Laws of the Russian Empire* [*Polnoe Sobranie Zakonov*, henceforth PSZ], Second collection, Vol. III, No. 1852, pgs. 219 and 101.

(6) Information and plate received from Cadet Corps.

(7) Information received from the Paul and 1st Moscow Cadet Corps.

(8) *Collection of Laws and Regulations*, 1829, Book IV, pg. 107.

(9) Ibid., pg. 115.

(10) Ibid., Book III, pgs. 79 et seq.

(11) Ibid., 1830, Book III, pg. 179.

(12) Ibid., 1831, Book IV, pg. 91.

(13) Ibid., 1832, Book I, pg. 173.

(14) Ibid., 1832, Book II, pg. 545.

(15) Ibid., Book IV, pgs. 140 et seq.

(16) Ibid., pg. 157.

(17) Ibid., 1833, Book I, pg. 575.

(18) Ibid., pg. 577.

(19) Ibid., pg. 419.

(20) Ibid., pg. 463.

(21) Ibid., pg. 469.

(22) Ibid., pg. 229.

(23) Ibid., 1834, Book II, pg. 93.

(24) Ibid., pg. 281.

(25) Ibid., Book III, pg. 465.

(26) Ibid., 1835, Book I, pg. 343.

(27) Information received from the Nobiliary Regiment.

(28) *Collection of Laws and Regulations*, 1835, Book III, pg. 179.

(29) Ibid., 1836, Book I, pg. 73.

(30) Ibid., Book II, pg. 209, and information received from Cadet Corps.

(31) *Collection of Laws and Regulations*, 1837, Book III, pg. 47.

(32) Ibid., Book IV, pg. 325.

(33) Ibid., 1838, Book I, pg. 361.

(34) Memorandum of the Minister of War to HIS IMPERIAL HIGHNESS the Commander of Military Educational Institutions, 9 June 1840, No. 7658.

(35) Order of the Minister of War, 2 January 1844, No. 1.

(36) Ditto, 9 May 1844, Nos. 63 and 64.

(37) Supplement to the Regulations for the Orenburg-Neplyuev Cadet Corps, confirmed by HIGHEST Authority 4/16 June 1844.

(38) Order of the Minister of War, 7 December 1844, No. 147.

(39) Ditto, 4 January 1845, No. 1.

(40) Ditto, 9 August 1845, No. 101.

(41) HIGHEST Confirmed Regulation for the Siberian Cadet Corps, 24 October/5 November 1845.

(42) Information received from the Headquarters of Military Educational Institutions.

(43) Memorandum of the State-Secretary, Actual Privy Counciler Longinov, to HIS IMPERIAL HIGHNESS the Commander of Military Educational Institutions, 29 January 1846, No. 28, and Order of the Commander of Military Educational Institutions, 8 February 1846, No. 693.

(44) Memorandum of the Minister of War to the Commander of Military Educational Institutions, 20 March 1847, No. 3083, and Order of the Commander of Military Educational Institutions, 11 April 1847, No. 846.

(45) Order of the Minister of War, 19 March 1847, No. 86, and Order of the Commander of Military Educational Institutions, 7 July 1847, No. 874.

(46) Order of the Commander of Military Educational Institutions, 11 December 1847, No. 918.

(47) Order of the Minister of War, 9 November 1849, No. 110, and Order of the Commander of Military Educational Institutions, 23 November 1849, No. 1133.

(48) Memorandum of the Minister of War to the Commander of Military Educational Institutions, 22 February 1851, No. 2118, instruction of the Minister of War to the War Ministry's Commissariat Department, 23 February 1851, No. 2140, and Order of the Commander of Military Educational Institutions, 9 March 1851, No. 1303.

(49) Order of the Commander of Military Educational Institutions, 7 January 1852, No. 1442.

(50) Memorandum of the Minister of War to the Commander of Military Educational Institutions, 1 April 1853, No. 3826, and Order of the Commander of Military Educational Institutions, 14 April 1853, No. 1708.

(51) Memorandum of the Minister of War to the Commander of Military Educational Institutions, 21 May 1853, No. 6421, and Order of the Commander of Military Educational Institutions, 8 June 1853, No. 1748.

(52) *Collection of Laws and Regulations*, 1826, Book I, pg. 105.

(53) Ibid., Book II, pg. 47.

(54) Ibid., 1827, Book I, pg. 3.

(55) Information and plate received from the Main Engineering School.

(56) *Collection of Laws and Regulations*, 1829, Book IV, pg. 115.

(57) Ibid., 1830, Book III, pg. 231.

(58) Ibid., pg. 179.

(59) Ibid., 1832, Book I, pg. 173.

(60) Ibid., Book II, pg. 545.

(61) Ibid., 1833, Book I, pg. 419.

(62) Ibid., pg. 463.

(63) Ibid., 1834, Book III, pg. 465.

(64) Ibid., 1835, Book III, pg. 179.

(65) Ibid., 1836, Book II, pg. 209, and information received from the Main Engineering School.

(66) *Collection of Laws and Regulations*, 1837, Book III, pg. 47.

(67) Ibid., Book IV, pg. 325.

(68) Order of the Minister of War, 2 January 1844, No. 1.

(69. Ditto, 9 May 1844, Nos. 63 and 64.

(70) Ditto, 4 January 1845, No. 1.

(71) Ditto, 9 August 1845, No. 101.

(72) *Collection of Laws and Regulations*, 1826, Book I, pg. 105.

(73) Ibid., Book II, pg. 47.

(74) Ibid., 1827, Book I, pg. 3.

(75) Information and plate received from the Artillery School.

(76) *Collection of Laws and Regulations*, 1829, Book IV, pg. 115.

(77) Ibid., 1830, Book III, pg. 179.

(78) Ibid., 1832, Book I, pg. 173.

(79) Ibid., Book II, pg. 545.

(80) Ibid., 1833, Book I, pg. 419.

(81) Ibid., pg. 463.

(82) Ibid., 1834, Book II, pg. 163.

(83) Ibid., Book III, pg. 465.

(84) Ibid., 1836, Book II, pg. 209, and information received from the Artillery School.

(85) *Collection of Laws and Regulations*, 1837, Book III, pg. 47.

(86) Ibid., Book IV, pg. 325.

(87) Order of the Minister of War, 2 January 1844, No. 1.

(88) Ditto, 9 May 1844, Nos. 63 and 64.

(89) Ditto, 4 January 1845, No. 1.

(90) Ditto, 9 August 1845, No. 101.

(91) Order of the Commander of Military Educational Institutions, 20 September 1849, No. 1113.

(92) Information received from the Corps of Pages, and HIGHEST Confirmed table, 24 February 1827 .

(93) Information and plate received from that Corps.

(94) PSZ, Second collection, Vol. III, No. 1852, pgs. 219 and 101.

(95) *Collection of Laws and Regulations*, 1829, Book IV, pg. 115.

(96) Ibid., 1830, Book III, pg. 179.

(97) Ibid., 1832, Book II, pg. 545.

(98) Instruction of the Chief Director of the Corps of Pages, Cadet Corps, and Nobiliary Regiment, 30 July 1832, No. 559.

(99) *Collection of Laws and Regulations*, 1833, Book I, pg. 419.

(100) Ibid., pg. 463.

(101) Ibid., 1834, Book III, pg. 465.

(102) Ibid., 1835, Book III, pg. 179.

(103) Ibid., 1837, Book III, pg. 47.

(104) Ibid., Book IV, pg. 325.

(105) Order of the Minister of War, 2 January 1844, No. 1.

(106) Ditto, 9 May 1844, Nos. 63 and 64.

(107) Ditto, 7 December 1844, No. 147.

(108) Ditto, 4 January 1845, No. 1.

(109) Ditto, 9 August 1845, No. 101.

(110) Order of the Commander of Military Educational Institutions, 16 November 1852, No. 1627.

(111) HIGHEST Confirmed Regulation for the School of Guards Officer Candidates and Cavalry Cadets, 15 October 1838, §§ 43, 54, and 55, and tables attached to this regulation.

(112) The tables referenced in the preceding note.

(113) *Collection of Laws and Regulations*, 1838, Book IV, pg. 245.

(114) Ibid., 1838, Book II, pg. 145.

(115) Order of the Minister of War, 2 January 1844, No. 1.

(116) Ditto, 9 May 1844, Nos. 63 and 64.

(117) Ditto, 7 December 1844, No. 147.

(118) Ditto, 4 January 1845, No. 1.

(119) Ditto, 9 August 1845, No. 101.

(120) HIGHEST Confirmed Regulation of 15 October 1838, §50.

(121) *Collection of Laws and Regulations*, 1826, Book I, pgs. 109 and 110, and pg. 107, point 5.

(122) Ibid., Book II, pgs. 75 and 76.

(123) Ibid., 1827, Book I, pg. 3, and information received from the War Ministry's Commissariat Department.

(124) *Collection of Laws and Regulations*, 1829, Book II, pg. 225.

(125) Ibid., pg. 5.

(126) Ibid., Book IV, pg. 115.

(127) Ibid., 1830, Book IV, pgs. 401.

(128) Ibid., 1831, Book II, pg. 39.

(129) Ibid., 1832, Book I, pg. 3.

(130) Ibid., Book II, pg. 545.

(131) Ibid., 1836, Book I, pg. 75.

(132) Ibid., 1837, Book III, pg. 47.

(133) Ibid., Book IV, pg. 325.

(134) Order of the Minister of War, 23 January 1841, No. 8.

(135) Ditto, 8 April 1843, No. 44.

(136) Ditto, 8 April 1843, No. 44, and model shabrack and saddlecloths preserved by the War Ministry's Commissariat Department.

(137) Order of the Minister of War, 2 January 1844, No. 1.

(138) Ditto, 13 August 1845, No. 104, and models preserved by the War Ministry's Commissariat Department.

(139) Order of the Minister of War, 6 October 1845, No. 124.

(140) Ditto, 9 January 1848, No. 8.

(141) Ditto, 21 September 1849, No. 89.

(142) Ditto, 27 September 1849, No. 97.

(143) Ditto, 13 October and 3 December 1849, Nos. 104 and 121.

(144) Ditto, 15 February 1850, No. 13.

(145) Ditto, 18 February 1854, No. 21.

(146) Ditto, 29 April 1854, No 53, and information received from the War Ministry's Commissariat Department.

(147) Evidence from contemporaries.

(148) *Collection of Laws and Regulations*, 1826, Book I, pg. 105, and evidence from contemporaries to this change in General-Adjutants and Aides-de-Camp.

(149) *Collection of Laws and Regulations*, 1826, Book II, pg. 76.

(150) Ibid., 1827, Book I, pg. 3.

(151) Information and model saddlecloths received from the War Ministry's Commissariat Department.

(152) *Collection of Laws and Regulations*, 1829, Book IV, pg. 115.

(153) Ibid., 1830, Book IV, pg. 401.

(154) Ibid., 1832, Book I, pg. 3.

(155) Ibid., Book II, pg. 545.

(156) Ibid., 1834, Book II, pg. 33.

(157) Ibid., 1836, Book II, pg. 213.

(158) Ibid., 1837, Book III, pg. 47.

(159) Ibid., Book VI, pg. 325.

(160) Order of the Minister of War, 23 January 1841, No. 8.

(161) Ditto, 18 April 1843, No. 51.

(162) Ditto, 2 January 1844, No. 1.

(163) Ditto, 1 December 1844, No. 144.

(164) Ditto, 4 January 1845, No. 1.

(165) Ditto, 6 October 1845, No. 124, pg. 4.

(166) Ditto, 2 May 1846, No. 79.

(167) Ditto, 6 June 1846, No. 95.

(168) Memorandum of the Minister of War to the Commander of the IMPERIAL Main Headquarters, 18 July 1846, No. 6455.

(169) Order of the Minister of War, 9 January 1848, No. 8.

(170) Ditto, 27 September 1849, No. 97.

(171) Ditto, 13 October and 3 December 1849, Nos. 104 and 121.

(172) Ditto, 15 February 1850, No. 13.

(173) Ditto, 18 February 1854, No. 21.

(174) Ditto, 29 April 1854, No 53.

(175) Collection of Laws and Regulations, 1828, Book II, pg. 287.

(176) Ibid., 1829, Book IV, pg. 115.

(177) Ibid., 1832, Book I, pg. 3.

(178) Ibid., Book II, pg. 545.

(179) Ibid., 1836, Book II, pg. 213.

(180) Ibid., 1837, Book III, pg. 47.

(181) Ibid., 1837, Book IV, pg. 325.

(182) Order of the Minister of War, 23 January 1841, No. 8.

(183) Ditto, 18 April 1843, No. 51.

(184) Ditto, 2 January 1844, No. 1.

(185) Ditto, 1 December 1844, No. 145.

(186) Ditto, 4 June 1845, No. 86.

(187) Ditto, 9 July 1846, No. 117.

(188) Ditto, 27 September 1849, No. 97.

(189) Ditto, 13 October and 3 December 1849, Nos. 104 and 121.

(190) Ditto, 15 February 1850, No. 13.

(191) Ditto, 29 April 1854, No. 53.

РИСУНКИ
ОДЕЖДЫ и ВООРУЖЕНІЯ
РОССІЙСКИХЪ
ВОЙСКЪ
1825-1855.

PLATES LIST OF ILLUSTRATIONS

933. Chamber-Pages, 1827-1852. *In ceremonial and parade uniforms.*

934. Chamber-Page, 1827-1852. *In undress coat.*

935. Pages, 1827-1852. *In ballroom dress, in greatcoat, and in ceremonial uniform.*

936. Chamber-Page and Page, 1827-1828. *In formation uniform.*

937. Pages, 1827-1832. *In everyday and field uniforms.*

938. Company-Grade Officer. Corps of Pages, 1827-1828.

939. Page, 1828-1833. *In formation uniform.*

940. Page, 1833-1844. *In formation uniform.*

941. Company-Grade Officer of the Corps of Pages, and Page, 1844-1855. *In formation uniform.*

942. Chamber-Page and Page, 1852-1855. *In parade and ceremonial uniforms.*

943. Page, 1852-1855. *In parade uniform.*

944. Officer Candidate [*Podpraporshchik*] and Company-Grade Officer. Company of the School for Guards Officer Candidates and Cadets, 1838-1844.

945. Company-Grade Officer. Squadron of the School for Guards Officer Candidates and Cadets, 1838-1844.

946. Cadet [*Yunker*]. Squadron of the School for Guards Officer Candidates and Cadets, 1838-1844.

947. Cadet and Officer Candidate. School for Guards Officer Candidates and Cadets, 1844-1855.

948. Field-Grade Officer. Company of the School for Guards Officer Candidates and Cadets, 1845-1855.

949. Infantry Generals, 1826-1845.

950. General. Light Cavalry in the Separate Lithuanian Corps, 1826-1829. *In undress coat.*

951. Garrison General, 1826-1844.

952. General. Light Cavalry, 1826-1845. *In undress coat.*

953. General-Field Marshal's epaulette, established 1 January 1827.

954. General. Heavy Cavalry, 1829-1845.

955. General. Heavy Cavalry, 1830-1845. *In undress coat.*

956. Shabrack, holster, and saddle for Generals of infantry and in the Guards Cuirassier Division, of the patterns confirmed 8 April 1843.

957. Saddlecloth for Generals of Army Heavy Cavalry, of the pattern confirmed 8 April 1843.

958. General Officer's helmet, established 13 August 1845. *(For Generals in the Guards Cavalry Corps.)*

959. Helmet plate for Army Generals, established 13 August 1845.

960. General, unattached in the Army, 1845-1855. *In undress coat.*

961. Infantry and Cavalry Generals. Separate Caucasus Corps, 1850-1855.

962. Cavalry General. Separate Caucasus Corps, 1850-1855. *In undress half-caftan.*

963. Aide-de-Camp's epaulette, established 14 December 1825.

964. Infantry General-Adjutant, 1826-1844.

965. Cavalry Aide-de-Camp, 1826-1844.

966. Campaign saddlecloth for General-Adjutants, established in 1828.

967. Cavalry Aide-de-Camp, 1844-1855.

968. Helmet plate for Aides-de-Camp, established 1 December 1844.

969. Infantry Aide-de-Camp, 1845-1849.

970. Cavalry General-Adjutant and Infantry AdC, unattached in the Separate Caucasus Corps, 1850-1855.

971. Infantry Aide-de-Camp, unattached in the Separate Caucasus Corps, 1850-1855. *In undress coat.*

972. Braided aiguilette knot, for use with Hussar uniforms, established 7 February 1852.

973. Infantry General-Adjutant, 1854-1855.

974. Cavalry and Infantry Generals of HIS IMPERIAL MAJESTY'S Suite, 1828-1845.

975. Infantry General of HIS IMPERIAL MAJESTY'S Suite, 1845-1855.

976. Cavalry General of HIS IMPERIAL MAJESTY'S Suite, in the Separate Caucasus Corps, 1850-1855.

Cadets [Kadety], 1st and 2nd Cadet corps. Pupil [Vospitannik], Nobiliary Regiment. 1826-1828.

Cadet, Moscow Cadet Corps. Pupil, Imperial Military Orphans' Home. 1826-1828.

Hornist. 1st Cadet Corps, 1826-1828.

896

Company-Grade Officers. 1st and 2nd Cadet Corps and Nobiliary Regiment, 1826-1828.

33

897

Field-Grade Officer. 1st Cadet Corps, 1826-1828.

34

898

Cadets. 1st and 2nd Cadet Corps, 1827-1828.

Cadet, 1st Cadet Corps, and Company-Grade Officer, Moscow Cadet Corps. 1828.

Company-Grade Officer and Cadet. Paul Cadet Corps, 1829-1833.

901

Field-Grade Officer. 2nd Cadet Corps, 1829-1844. (Note: in 1830 the rapier sword was replaced by a half-saber.)

902

Cadet and Company-Grade Officer. Finland Cadet Corps, 1830-1833.

903

Sergeant [fel dfebel]. Moscow Cadet Corps, 1831-1833.

40

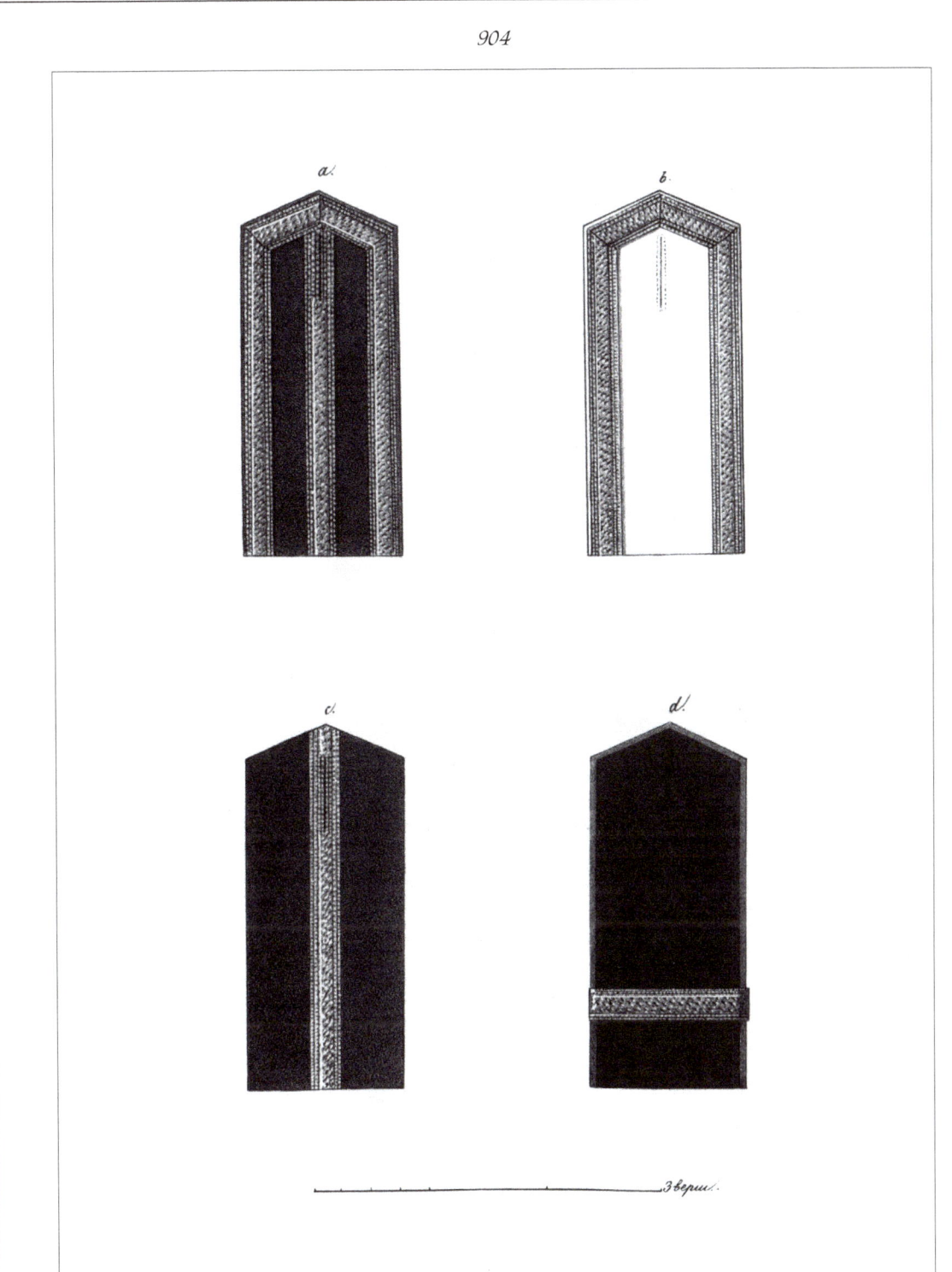

a.

б.

c.

d.

3 верш.

Shoulder straps of Military Educational Institutions, with rank distinctions, established 16 December 1831. a. Sergeant. b. Senior non-commissioned officer. c. Junior non-commissioned officer. d. Lance-corporal.

Cadets. Alexander Young Boys' Cadet Corps, 1832-1846.

Company-Grade Officer, 1st Cadet Corps. Non-Commissioned Officer, Nobiliary Regiment. 1833-1844.

Company-Grade Officer, 2nd Cadet Corps. Cadet, Moscow Cadet Corps. 1833-1835.

908

Cadet. 1st Cadet Corps, 1834-1844. In field dress.

909

Cadet, 1st Cadet Corps, and Non-Commissioned Officer, Nobiliary Regiment, attached to the Model Cavalry Regiment and Model Horse-Artillery Battery. 1835-1840.

910

Pupils from mountain tribes. Military Educational Institutions, 1835-1855. In parade and everyday dress.

Muslim pupils. Military Educational Institutions, 1833-1855. In everyday and parade dress.

912

Company-Grade Officer. Nobiliary Regiment, 1835-1844.

913

Field-Grade Officer. Paul Cadet Corps, 1844-1855.

Field-Grade Officer, 1st Cadet Corps, and Pupil, Nobiliary Regiment. 1844-1855.

Drummer. 2nd Cadet Corps, 1844-1855.

916

Cadets. Orenburg-Neplyuev Cadet Corps, 1844-1855.

917

Field-Grade Officer. Orenburg-Neplyuev Cadet Corps, 1844-1847.

918

Field-Grade Officer. 2nd Cadet Corps, 1845-1849.

55

Company-Grade Officer and Cadet. Siberian Cadet Corps squadron, 1845-1855.

920

Cadet. Alexander Young Boys' Cadet Corps, 1846-1855.

921

Company-Grade Officer. Orenburg-Neplyuev Cadet Corps, 1847-1855.

Company-Grade Officer's epaulette and cadet's shoulder strap for the Poltava Cadet Corps, established 9 March 1851.

Conductor and Company-Grade Officer. Main Engineering School, 1826-1828.

924

Conductor. Main Engineering School, 1828-1833.

925

Conductor. Main Engineering School, 1833-1844.

Company-Grade Officer and Non-Commissioned Officer. Main Engineering School, 1844-1855.

927

Cadet [Yunker] and Company-Grade Officer. Artillery School, 1826-1828.

Company-Grade Officer. Artillery School, 1828-1830.

929

Cadet. Artillery School, 1833-1844.

930

Cadet. Artillery School, 1844-1849.

Company-Grade Officer. Artillery School, 1845-1849.

Company-Grade Officer's epaulette and cadet's shoulder strap for the Michael Artillery School, established 20 September 1849.

933

Chamber-Pages, 1827-1852. In ceremonial and parade uniforms.

70

934

Chamber-Page, 1827-1852. In undress coat.

Pages, 1827-1852. In ballroom dress, in greatcoat, and in ceremonial uniform.

936

Chamber-Page and Page, 1827-1828. In formation uniform.

Pages, 1827-1832. In everyday and field uniforms.

938

Company-Grade Officer. Corps of Pages, 1827-1828.

Page, 1828-1833. In formation uniform.

940

Page, 1833-1844. In formation uniform.

Company-Grade Officer of the Corps of Pages, and Page, 1844-1855. In formation uniform.

942

Chamber-Page and Page, 1852-1855. In parade and ceremonial uniforms.

943

Page, 1852-1855. In parade uniform.

944

Officer Candidate [Podpraporshchik] and Company-Grade Officer. Company of the School for Guards Officer Candidates and Cadets, 1838-1844.

945

Company-Grade Officer. Squadron of the School for Guards Officer Candidates and Cadets, 1838-1844.

82

946

Cadet [Yunker]. Squadron of the School for Guards Officer Candidates and Cadets, 1838-1844.

Cadet and Officer Candidate. School for Guards Officer Candidates and Cadets, 1844-1855.

Field-Grade Officer. Company of the School for Guards Officer Candidates and Cadets, 1845-1855.

Infantry Generals, 1826-1845.

General. Light Cavalry in the Separate Lithuanian Corps, 1826-1829. In undress coat.

951

Garrison General, 1826-1844.

952

General. Light Cavalry, 1826-1845. In undress coat.

953

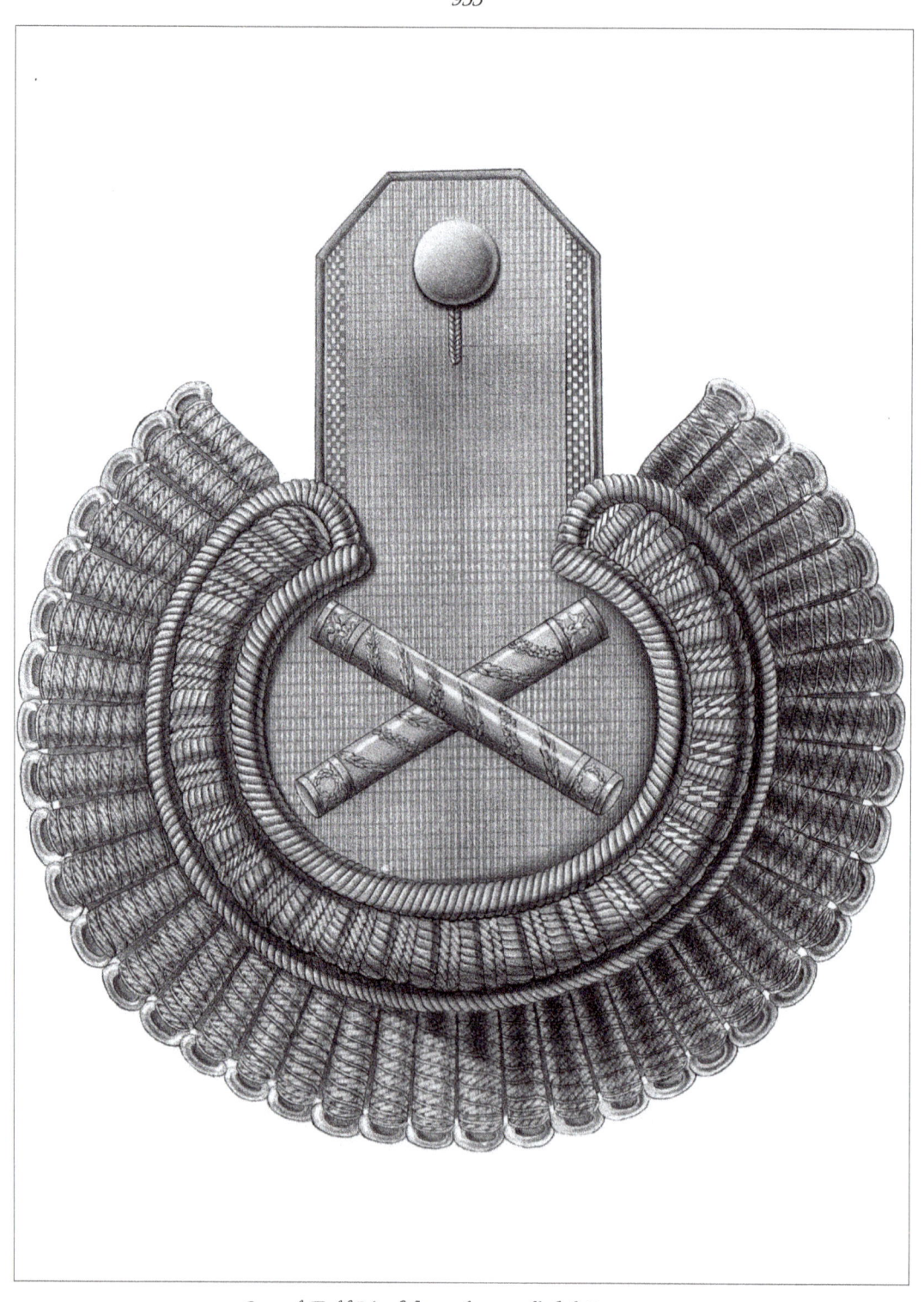

General-Field Marshal's epaulette, established 1 January 1827.

954

General. Heavy Cavalry, 1829-1845.

955

General. Heavy Cavalry, 1830-1845. In undress coat.

Shabrack, holster, and saddle for Generals of infantry and in the Guards Cuirassier Division, of the patterns confirmed 8 April 1843.
Saddlecloth for Generals of Army Heavy Cavalry, of the pattern confirmed 8 April 1843.

General Officer's helmet, established 13 August 1845. (For Generals in the Guards Cavalry Corps.)

959

Helmet plate for Army Generals, established 13 August 1845.

General, unattached in the Army, 1845-1855. In undress coat.

961

Infantry and Cavalry Generals. Separate Caucasus Corps, 1850-1855.

Cavalry General. Separate Caucasus Corps, 1850-1855. In undress half-caftan.

963

Aide-de-Camp's epaulette, established 14 December 1825.

964

Infantry General-Adjutant, 1826-1844.

965

Cavalry Aide-de-Camp, 1826-1844.

Campaign saddlecloth for General-Adjutants, established in 1828.

967

Cavalry Aide-de-Camp, 1844-1855.

Helmet plate for Aides-de-Camp, established 1 December 1844.

969

Infantry Aide-de-Camp, 1845-1849.

Cavalry General-Adjutant and Infantry Aide-de-Camp, unattached in the Separate Caucasus Corps, 1850-1855.

971

Infantry Aide-de-Camp, unattached in the Separate Caucasus Corps, 1850-1855. In undress coat.

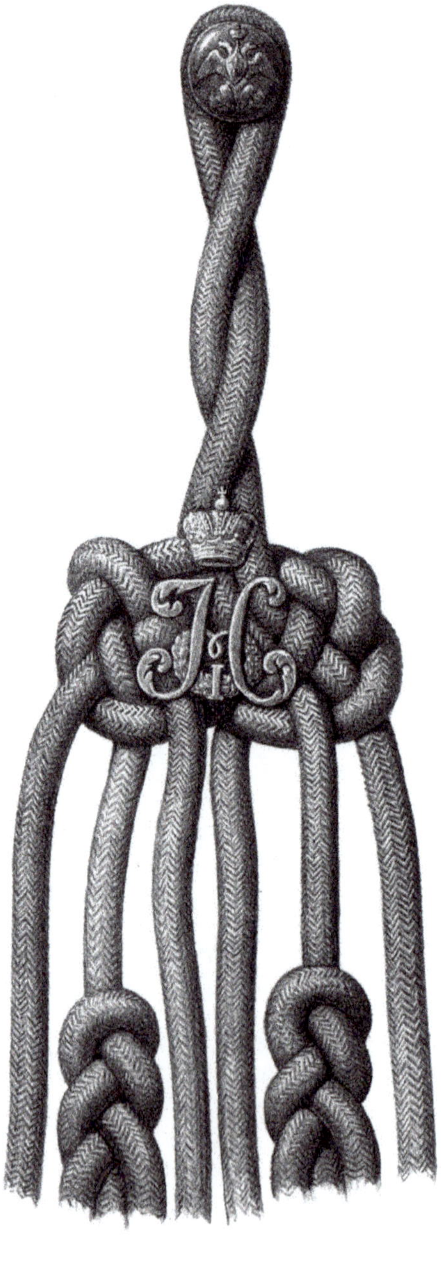

Braided aiguilette knot [Aksel bantnyi naplechnyi zhgut], for use with Hussar uniforms, established 7 February 1852.

973

Infantry General-Adjutant, 1854-1855.

974

Cavalry and Infantry Generals of HIS IMPERIAL MAJESTY'S Suite, 1828-1845.

975

Infantry General of HIS IMPERIAL MAJESTY'S Suite, 1845-1855.

976

Cavalry General of HIS IMPERIAL MAJESTY'S Suite, in the Separate Caucasus Corps, 1850-1855.

112

SOLDIERS, WEAPONS & UNIFORMS ALREADY PUBLISHED
(SOME TITLES)

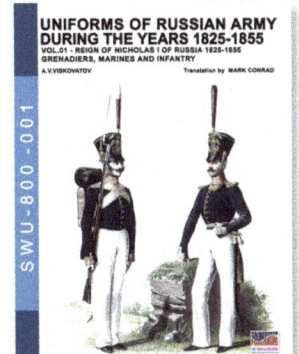
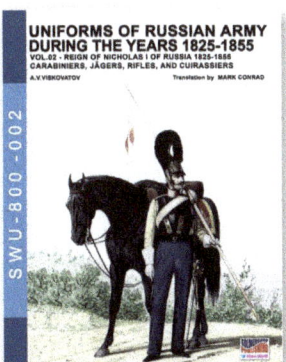
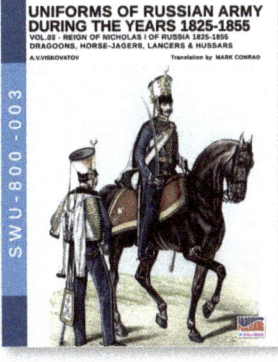
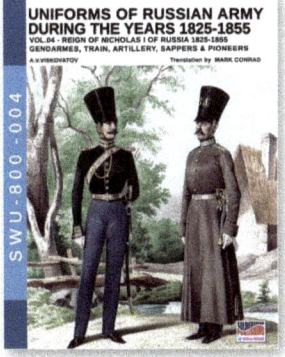

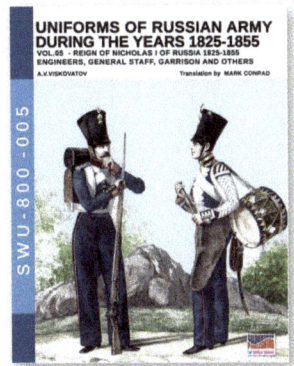
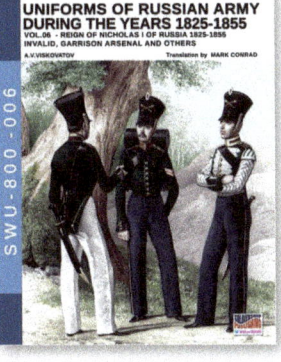

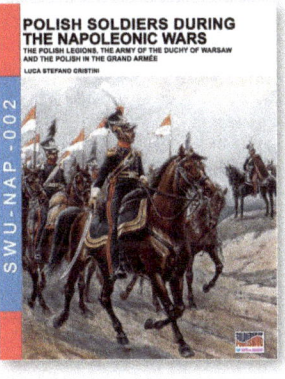
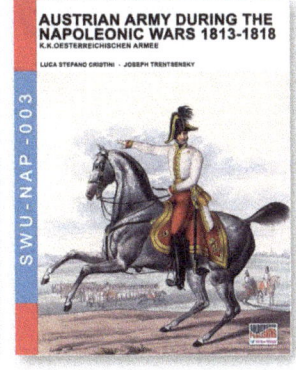
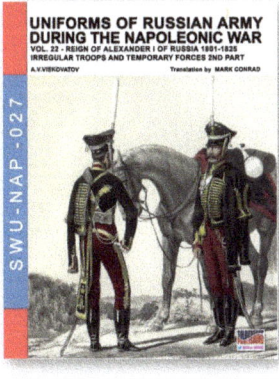